BRUNO MARS

BRUNO MARS

EMILY HERBERT

OMNIBUS PRESS

London / New York / Paris / Sydney / Copenhagen / Berlin / Madrid / Tokyo

Exclusive Distributors
Music Sales Limited,
14/15 Berners Street,
London, W1T 3LJ.

Music Sales Corporation
180 Madison Avenue, 24th Floor,
New York,
NY 10016,
USA.

Macmillan Distribution Services
56 Parkwest Drive
Derrimut, Vic 3030,
Australia.

Every effort has been made to trace the copyright holders of the photographs in this book but one or
two were unreachable. We would be grateful if the photographers concerned would contact us.

Typeset by Phoenix Photosetting, Chatham, Kent
Printed in the EU

A catalogue record for this book is available from the British Library.

Visit Omnibus Press on the web at www.omnibuspress.com

CONTENTS

Chapter 1

White Lines And Conspiracy Theories

L as Vegas, 2010. The most famous entertainment capital in the world was in full swing: packed with tourists visiting the luxury hotels, the resort was alive to the sound of music, of gambling, of partying and having fun. This was the place that attracted the A list of the A list: right back from the fifties, when the Rat Pack – Frank Sinatra, Dean Martin and Sammy Davis Jr – made it the hippest place to be, to the seventies, when Elvis made it his home away from home, and now a whole new generation of entertainers was drawing in the crowds. Elton John, Cher and Celine Dion were just three of the massive stars who had recently enjoyed lengthy residencies at the famous resort in the Nevada desert and now a whole host of newcomers was looking to join them.

Everywhere you looked the city was bustling with pleasure seekers, out for a good time, some on a weekend break, others using the bright lights and sense of unreality to forget about troubles back home. Household names were everywhere you looked. The famous Las Vegas Strip was home to some of the most famous hotels in the world: Caesars Palace, the Palazzo, the Venetian, the Mirage, Bellagio, Encore, Wynn, Casino Royale – they were all here. Shoppers, spectators, hardened gamblers, thrill seekers, fun lovers crowded the sidewalks of the city, vast multi-cultural throngs of people in a sea of neon, gathered in Vegas from all over the world. On one section of the Strip, the famous Bellagio fountain shot jets of water high into the sky, seemingly weaving and dancing to the music. Elsewhere in the town were more household names: the Golden Nugget, the Freemont, the California and the Plaza. This was the city that never slept, a monument to hedonism, America's favourite fun palace.

As the glittering bars, restaurants, theatres and casinos continued to draw in the crowds, people were drinking, smoking, taking in the shows and above all, gambling. This was party town and the crowds were partying hard. And that applied to the entertainers just as much as it did to the punters, leading to one incident that was to make headlines all over the world. The Hard Rock Hotel & Casino was a relative newcomer in town, built in 1995 by Peter Morton, co-founder of the Hard Rock Café and extensively refurbished in 2010: perhaps its most notable feature was, appropriately enough, a prominent Fender Stratocaster guitar, lodged in the hotel's roof.

As well as the usual casino, the Hard Rock Hotel & Casino featured a rock club called The Joint, where numerous musical luminaries had performed in the past, including David Bowie, Guns N' Roses, Coldplay, Oasis and the Rolling Stones. The hotel also housed Vanity nightclub, Rehab, a massive outdoor pool party at the hotel's Beach Club, various restaurants, shops and spas. It had already featured in the public eye several times in the past, not only through appearances in the films *Con Air*, *Vegas Vacation* and *Honey, I Blew Up The Kid*, but also because John

Entwistle of the Who died in one of its rooms in 2002. Scandal was the life blood of rock 'n' roll; it was hardly surprising, then, that a hotel built to celebrate rock should have its own brushes with notoriety, courtesy of some of its livelier guests.

But one scandal threatened to derail the career of a promising performer almost before it had begun. It was breaking news: there was trouble at the Hard Rock Hotel & Casino. Early one Sunday morning, an attendant in the men's room suspected a young man in situ was using cocaine – he had gone into one of the stalls in the loos and had not come out for an awfully long time. He called the hotel security staff, who detained the young man while calling the police – he could "see a male in a striped red shirt with a baggy [sic] of white powder substance", the attendant said. Arrests were made when the young man, one Peter Hernandez, was found to be in possession of 2.6 grams of the white powder – the police asked him to "give over whatever narcotics he had". Reasoning that his best bet was to do just that, according to the police report, Peter "pulled out a white powder substance, which was consistent with cocaine, from his left-front jeans pocket". Clearly panicking, Peter asked, "Can I speak to you honestly sir?" and "admitted he did a foolish thing and has never used drugs before". With that, Peter was hauled off to a holding cell in the county jail and booked on suspicion of possession of a controlled substance.

But this was no ordinary tale of a young man running a little wild on a trip to Las Vegas for Peter had actually been performing at the Hard Rock earlier. Nor was he commonly known as Peter Hernandez, although that was his real name. Rather, he was increasingly making waves, first as a songwriter and more recently as a singer, under the moniker Bruno Mars. The timing could not have been worse: he had been attracting attention from the industry, to say nothing of very favourable reviews, for his work on B.o.B.'s 'Nothin' On You', which had got to number one on the *Billboard* Hot 100, the song he wrote for CeeLo, 'Fuck You', and now his own first single, 'Just The Way You Are', which had also made its debut in the charts. It is one thing having an established star up on a drugs charge, but quite another for a relative newcomer to get caught up in a crisis before he's even had a chance to show what's he's made of. It could have been over for Bruno before he had even begun. In the event, however, he was extremely lucky: his record label stood behind him. "We congratulate Bruno Mars on his chart topping success and provide him with our full love and support," said a spokesman for Elektra. So that was OK. Bruno wasn't going to lose the recording contract he'd fought so long and so hard to make his own.

But what really happened that night in Las Vegas? Bruno has since hinted that, no matter what he told the police, this was not the first time he'd tried drugs, and there are some people in his circle who are convinced that the official version of events is not the whole story. Indeed, the whole episode threw up a series of mysteries that to this day have never been fully explained. The first was the ongoing suspicion that Bruno had been set up. He may well have been unwise, foolish and a lawbreaker, but Bruno is, by a long shot, not the first young entertainer to take cocaine when out on the road, especially not in Las Vegas. To this day, there are those who believe that one of the security guards in the Hard Rock Café saw Bruno, gave him the drugs, waited for him to visit the men's room and then alerted the police himself. Others believe that it was one of Bruno's own circle, in his set of hangers-on.

No one has ever been able to prove this, but it is certainly the case that the relevant people involved knew exactly where to find him, right down to which cubicle of which men's room he was in. Bruno had learned the hard way that when your star begins to rise, there are plenty of people willing to take you down a peg or two and that includes those you thought you could trust and who put themselves forward as a friend. It was a harsh introduction to his new reality: he was on the verge of mega-stardom, but that could be dangerous territory, fraught not only with temptation, but with people who were actively seeking to do you down.

Bruno had to accept this and, behind the scenes, his lawyers got to work to minimise the damage. His growing profile might have counted against him, if someone decided he should be made an example of, but at the same time, he was a young man with no previous convictions who had committed a non-violent offence. If Bruno showed contrition, accepted his wrongdoing – which, to his credit, he did right from the start – and showed that he really would not be repeating the error, there was a good chance that he would get off with a fine and community service, rather than a jail sentence. Strangely enough, these were exactly the circumstances that were to apply to someone else involved in the case, who was treated far more harshly than Bruno was to be, of which more later on.

That Bruno and his record label were taking this pretty seriously was underlined when they hired Blair Berk, of Tarlow & Berk, to handle the case. Something of a legend in celebrity circles, Blair was a Harvard Law School graduate from North Carolina who made her name in the early nineties when Ozzy Osbourne was named in a civil suit when his song lyrics were blamed for the suicide of a teenager from the state of Georgia. Blair listened to the tape, realised it had been remixed by the record company and got the case thrown out before it went to trial. Since then she had represented Gerard Butler and Kayne West when they were involved in a fight with paparazzi, Reese Witherspoon after an assault at Disneyland, and Heather Locklear, Kiefer Sutherland, Queen Latifah and Lindsay Lohan, all of whom were arrested for driving under the influence.

Utterly unimpressed by her starry clientele, Blair was the perfect lawyer for a celebrity to turn to in a crisis: "If it was Washington, I would have defended congressmen," she once said of working in Los Angeles. "If it was Detroit, it would have been car executives. I come onto a case in the midst of a crisis and I have absolutely no interest in having a relationship with my client. I'm not interested in making a movie with them. I have no agenda. If I wanted to be a movie star, I'd be a movie star." She also observed on another occasion, "I think in this celebrity-obsessed culture we lose sight of how human and vulnerable we all are when we're in crisis. It must be very daunting to be someone who has fame but doesn't have someone to trust." Bruno, who had family and friends, was not exactly in this position, of course, but he was certainly becoming aware of trust issues. And if there was anyone who would be able to get him out of his current mess it was Blair.

And so, as the lawyers worked out the best way to handle this, Bruno's court date was initially set for December 14, 2010. This was then pushed back to the next year, February 14, 2011. Bruno initially appeared in court on February 4, 2011, soberly dressed in a dark suit and tie, looking much younger than his years. He had three defence lawyers at his side. Looking very nervous, he confirmed that his name was Peter Hernandez and agreed not to contest the police report that stated he was in possession of 2.6 grams of cocaine when he was arrested at a Vegas club last September. He would plead guilty, he said. Given the evidence against him, he didn't have much choice, but even so, this was working in Bruno's favour. Had there been any attempt to wiggle out of it, the prosecutors and judge might well have decided to throw the book at him. If Bruno had been set up, then at least he was dealing with it in the wisest way possible.

But the awkwardness of the time was being underlined by the fact that Bruno was living two lives simultaneously – one in which he was being had up in court on possession of drugs and the other in which he was turning into an international star. The hearing was set for February 14, and while that meant at least it would be over pretty quickly, slightly awkwardly, the Grammy awards were being held the night before. Bruno was up for seven of these gongs, including best male pop vocal for 'Just The Way You Are', but what should have been his moment of triumph now risked being overshadowed by the prospect of disgrace. Bruno was aware of that, but there was nothing that could be done: he had to take the rap and it was better just to get on with it. And so, on February 13, 2011, at the 53rd Grammy awards at the Staples Center in Los Angeles, broadcast to over 26 million people, Bruno won the Best Male Pop Vocal Performance, beating Michael Bublé, Michael Jackson (a posthumous release of 'This Is It'), Adam Lambert and John Mayer, a sort of pop coronation of the major new talent on the scene.

But it was a very different scene the following day. Back in Las Vegas, as expected, in return for pleading guilty, Bruno was let off relatively lightly. He was told he would have to pay a $2,000 fine, do 200 hours of community service and complete a drug counselling course of eight hours, and if all that went according to plan and he managed to stay out of trouble, then in due course, the charges would be expunged from his record. "We're extremely pleased the charge against Bruno is going to be dismissed," said Blair, adding that the judge had taken into account the fact that this was Bruno's first offence.

The community service was to be with various children's and health-related charities based in Los Angeles and Minneapolis on efforts including charity videos and concerts, an anti-bullying campaign (a cause close to Bruno's heart, of which more anon) and much else. And while it might not have seemed so at the time, this might also have been exactly the counterbalance that Bruno needed as his star continued to rise. Many a young singer gets carried away with his own publicity (indeed, that might well have been exactly what led to the cocaine incident) and so to continue in his increasingly successful career while at the same time working with less privileged people would have kept Bruno's feet firmly on the ground. Yes, he was on his way, but there were some people considerably less fortunate than him who he was going to be working with at close quarters. It was going to do him no harm at all.

But the ramifications of this curious case continued to spread. Blair was not the only high-profile lawyer to have been involved: the prosecutor was a well-respected lawyer called David Schubert, who had spent 10 years as a Clark County prosecutor, including a stint as a liaison to a federal drug task force. Bruno was not his only prominent drugs prosecution: he had also been involved in the case of Paris Hilton, although she was treated more severely than Bruno, admitting to two misdemeanours and getting a year's probation. No one, including his girlfriend (he was divorced and his ex-wife and two teenage children had moved to another state) had had any idea that Schubert himself had a serious drug abuse problem and so it came as a shock when, just one month after Bruno's trial, Schubert was himself arrested. Then 47, he was pulled over at about 5pm one Saturday afternoon and swallowed a crack rock as an undercover policeman closed in; however, a second rock was later found in his car. In total he was in possession of $40 worth of crack cocaine. An unregistered handgun was also in his car.

It was apparent right away that Schubert was going to be treated with nothing like the lenience Bruno was. For a start, this was not a one-off: the street dealer, from whom Schubert had bought the drugs, told the police that Schubert had started buying six or seven months previously, and scored three or four times a week. Clark County District Attorney David Roger gave an early signal the law was about to come down on him like a ton of bricks: "It's disheartening. Obviously I don't expect any of our prosecutors to be using drugs, but I was especially shocked he was buying crack cocaine to smoke it," he told the *NY Daily News*. "I placed a great deal of trust in him, assigning him to a state and federal drug task force. I have zero tolerance. We're moving forward with his termination."

Schubert was duly forced to resign, setting in motion a chain of events that was to end in tragedy. The authorities got warrants to check his blood and his two residences and his decline began immediately. The shame of what had happened and the ending of his career began to take its toll and while the authorities could have adopted a sympathetic attitude towards a decent man who had developed a terrible addiction, they did not. Schubert's case could not have been helped by the fact that some people immediately began to comment on the leniency of Bruno's sentence: could it be, they asked, that he got off lightly because the prosecutor was himself a drug user? In actual fact it was the judge in the case, not the prosecutor, who pronounced sentence, and Bruno got almost exactly what anyone else would have got in the circumstances. He just happened to have a famous name.

Schubert could have expected the same – indeed, he did. As a first-time, non-violent offender, he could have expected probation (which is what Bruno got), but instead had the book thrown at him. The judge called him "a disgrace to his oath as a prosecutor and a lawyer" and sentenced him to a year to 30 months in prison, of which he served five months, after initially fleeing to Mexico when he learned that the Nevada Supreme Court had temporarily suspended his licence, and then returning, when he accepted the inevitable, that he would have to pay his dues. In prison, he was isolated for his own protection, having himself been a prosecutor. People familiar with the case said that this would break him and they were right: "I did what I did and I accept the consequences," he told the *Las Vegas Review-Journal* in a jailhouse interview. "But I don't feel I was treated fairly by the system."

After his release, matters went from bad to worse. Money troubles began to pile up as one of his properties was repossessed, and he began drinking heavily – all this, of course, in sight of the state parole officers who were looking after him and whom he would have known previously in a professional capacity. He split up from his girlfriend, Marian Kamalani, a legal colleague, and his behaviour towards her degenerated to the extent that she was forced to apply for a protective order from the courts. Her application gave an insight into quite how far he had fallen from grace: his entire life had become consumed with hatred of District Judge Carolyn Ellsworth, the judge who had treated him so harshly, and desperately tried to get the sentence repealed.

"The entire relationship was plagued by insanity and madness," Kamalani wrote. "I feel he is still angry at the world because of the outcome of his case. While we lived and worked together for nine months, the case dictated the course of the relationship. It was the topic of conversation – and we were consumed by one thing – not letting the District Court judge win. There were times when it seemed that a victory was possible through writs that were filed with the Supreme Court, and during those times everything was fine. But when the case was dealt huge blows, everything went to hell and it went to hell really fast."

This story reached a terrible denouement when, aged 49, Schubert took his own life in July 2013. To many this was a tragic inevitability: Schubert had sown the seeds of his own destruction, but although some reached out to try to help him, the legal system did not. There were suggestions that they were ashamed that this had happened to one of their own – and that even worse, while taking the drugs, Schubert was still able to function as a high-flying lawyer – but whatever the case, it was clear that his steep decline was known about. "I had some concerns about

Dave's conduct, and I had several conversations with Parole and Probation in an effort to get Dave some help," said Louis Schneider, a fellow attorney who had worked with Schubert to try to get the sentence repealed, and also a friend, talking to the *Las Vegas Review-Journal*. "I don't know what Probation did after those conversations."

Why could no one help someone who had clearly been a very troubled man? His death sparked a wave of guilt and anger through the community and the strength of this was signalled when Professor Mary Berkheiser, with whom Schubert had studied at the University of Nevada, Las Vegas (UNLV), sent out an email to colleagues in the wake of his death, which seemed to imply that Schubert was actually too sympathetic a man to be a good prosecutor.

"David was such a decent, good man who made me proud to have been a part of his life at Boyd [the William S Boyd School of Law at UNLV], and I want us all to remember him completely and take what lessons we can from his life both here at Boyd and beyond," she wrote. He was a "fierce advocate for the rights of his young clients" at her clinic, causing her to wonder whether he really was suited for being a prosecutor. Schubert graduated from law school in 2001 and a few years later emailed to say he was glad he had taken her course. He said it helped him "be more understanding of those he was prosecuting and not always go for the jugular in seeking the toughest possible penalty."

She was not alone in thinking that Schubert was a good man who had been treated badly. "Without question, David was treated differently than others charged with first-time drug offences," said former Clark County DA David Roger in an interview with *Las Vegas Citylife*, in stark contrast to his initial anger. "The criminal justice system focuses on rehabilitating drug users when they first enter the system. Unfortunately, David was not afforded that same understanding and compassion by the system in which he worked."

It was a sad end to a sad story. In January 2012, it was deemed that Bruno had served his debt to society and it was announced that after meeting the terms of his plea deal, the slate was to be wiped clean and that he would avoid a conviction for cocaine possession. In fact, he had more than wiped the slate clean. Although he was sentenced to 200 hours of community service, in actual fact he did more than 230, a sure sign that he was determined to put it all behind him and make up for what he had done. The guilty plea was taken off his record. Despite the fact that he was by now a huge star, Bruno had wisely remained silent about the episode, a silence that he finally broke in 2013.

His confession, as it were, appeared in *GQ* magazine, in whose pages he finally opened up about what had happened that night. For a start, he dropped some heavy hints that not only had that not been his first time using the drug, but that he had a potential problem with cocaine, though he was keen to emphasise that this was completely behind him and that he now lived a clean life.

Even so, Bruno appeared to think that he should be cut a little slack. He hadn't been the first to do this and he sure wasn't going to be the last: "I was young, man! I was in fucking Vegas. I wasn't thinking," he said. "I was really drunk. So a lot of that is a big blur, and I try every day to forget and keep pushing." And so he had become a new man.

The incident, though, had been a frightening wake-up call: it had taken Bruno years to get as far as he had done at the point of the arrest, and this was a graphic reminder that good fortune can quickly turn sour. When asked what he'd learned from the whole episode, he replied, "'I can take this shit away from you, young man.' That was the lesson. You've slaved away for years and years and years. You've prepped your whole life. It's all you know how to do. You're a kid experiencing life in fucking Sin City, and that was the lesson: it can all be taken away. Put you in a weird place. Embarrass you." It could be taken away but it hadn't been.

Now that Bruno was willing to talk about it, however, he opened up quite a bit more. "Oh yeah, of course," when asked if he'd felt scared. "I was given a number one record and I'm out doing dumb shit." As for telling the police it was his first time – "I don't know where that came from," he said. "I was really intoxicated. Of course, being so high profile he hadn't been allowed to forget – every court appearance brought immense media scrutiny, something else that Bruno had had to learn to get used to.

There was also some good-natured mockery to take on board. Bruno had had to take some stick on the subject of his mug shot: while most celebrities who get caught in an compromising situation tend to adopt a pained and strained expression, Bruno was pictured with a beaming smile. What was that all about then? "I don't know... it was a picture," he said somewhat lamely. And it was a picture that would return to haunt him from time to time. Despite having been in a very difficult situation, Bruno had come out of it with his reputation, if anything, enhanced. He had been totally honest in talking about the experience, and admitting he was scared that his good fortune might be taken away from him made him seem human and vulnerable.

And the issue continues to dog him to this day. Googling "Bruno Mars drugs" produces nearly eight million hits. It is something that Bruno has continued to be asked about, unfairly, really, because in an industry known for its heavy drug use, he, a minor offender compared to some, is still the poster boy for getting caught. But to his very great credit, Bruno continued to acknowledge quite how foolish he'd been – and that he really had risked losing it all. Neither did he ever show any signs of getting snappy with an interviewer for raising the subject, or indeed getting tired of talking about it, despite the fact that he'd gone over the same ground time and again.

"Yes, very stupid of me," he said in an interview with a Dutch fanzine, which is roughly translated here. "That incident is still following me till today. I can work as hard as I want and bring out 10 beautiful singles, [but] my using of drugs is something people will remember of me. And that's terrible. I want to continue with my life, forget what happened that day and show it's just all about music. I was a dumbass who wasn't thinking. My album was at number one and that success kinda went to my head. I drank too much that night and what happened next, I can't really remember. It was the first time I got in touch with drugs. I don't really understand why I did it and how I got it. When I got caught, I realised what the consequences would be. Fortunately, I came away from it with a community service and a fine."

And he was keen to emphasise that that was it when it came to drug taking. That part of his life was over. "I was living a good life," Bruno continued, talking of the period after the sentence had been made. "I also don't give wild parties at home. When I finish work, I watch some television or I go to bed. Or I play with my dog, Geronimo, a rottweiler." In other words, he had learned to cherish domesticity and had to a certain extent settled down – although that wasn't the whole story. Bruno was pretty good at writing mischievous song lyrics, and he also had quite an eye for the ladies, attracting many stunning ones, including his long term girlfriend, of which more anon. He was lucky – it could have been a lot worse, as it had been for one of the high-profile lawyers who had been involved in the case.

It was a salutary lesson, but Bruno had taken it on board. Unlike poor David Schubert, he had been given a second chance and it was one that he was very happy to take, as his star began to rocket globally and this young boy from Hawaii began to become famous all over the world. Bruno was fast becoming one of the most famous singers on the planet, garnering a huge fanbase, and acclaim as an exciting new singer/songwriter. And he was loving every minute, to boot. So just who was this young singing sensation? Where did he come from and how was he making such an impact?

Chapter 2

Little Elvis

Honolulu, Hawaii, and the Hernandez household was alive with the sound of music. There was no change there: it always was. Peter Hernandez and Bernadette "Bernie" San Pedro Bayot were one of the most musical couples in the whole of Hawaii, and their families were too: they even met because of music. The couple had encountered each other some years previously while performing in a show, where Bernie was a hula dancer and Peter played percussion: love, marriage and children followed, and music played in the background all the while.

And Honolulu was a lively place to grow up. The capital of Hawaii, with a lush, tropical climate, spectacularly beautiful surrounding scenery and Pacific Ocean setting, Honolulu was a cosmopolitan place, attracting visitors from all over the world. With a thriving arts scene, tourists in abundance and as the birthplace of many notables including Barack Obama, Nicole Kidman and Bette Midler, Honolulu was the ideal place to raise a family, especially one that was so heavily involved in the musical scene. Initially, at least, the couple were happy, settling into the multi-cultural American melting pot.

It was a multi-cultural family, too. Peter is half Puerto Rican and half Jewish (from Hungary and the Ukraine) and was born in Brooklyn before moving to Hawaii, while Bernie, born on August 21, 1957, of both Filipino and Spanish descent, had emigrated from the Philippines as a child in 1968, having previously lived in Baclaran, just south of Manila. She attended Farrington High School and after leaving became a lead dancer for Al Harrington's show. The couple were typical of modern-day Hawaii, with both born outside to families of differing ethnic origins and blending their backgrounds to create a future for themselves. After the marriage, the house was filled with music and children, of which there were to be six in total. It was a lively, happy family about to be made even livelier and happier by the arrival of the couple's fourth child.

On October 8, 1985, the Fernandez household was wildly excited: Bernie had just gone into labour with their next child, Peter Gene Hernandez, who would enter a world dominated by music as part of their growing family. He had one brother, Eric (Peter's son from a previous marriage, although Bernie raised him as her own), and four sisters, Jaime "Kailani", Tiara, Tahiti and Presley. Initially it was a peripatetic existence: the family moved around Oahu, living in Pearl City, Hawaii Kai and Palolo, before finally settling in Makiki, where Peter was to spend most of his childhood.

The young Peter was a lively baby, a livelier toddler and a born entertainer. With so much music around him, it entered his blood, becoming as much a part of his life as eating, breathing and speaking. Peter Jnr was fed music the way other babies are fed food: it was an integral part of his life, all-encompassing and very important. His siblings were equally musical: as he grew from a baby to a toddler, everyone around him was singing and dancing. Little Peter's life was mapped out before he even left the cradle.

Not that he was to be Peter Jnr for long. He was still just a toddler when he acquired a different name, one that has stuck to him ever since, and all because he was a little plump and bore a striking resemblance to a wrestler called Bruno Sammartino. Peter Snr thought this was too good not to use, and so he nicknamed his little boy "Bruno". Bruno, as he was thenceforth to be known, was very good-natured about it as an adult, treating the whole thing as a huge joke. "Oh, my dad nicknamed me 'Bruno' when I was two years old!" he told bluesandsoul.com. "You know, I guess I was this chubby kid, and at the time there was this chubby (Italian) wrestler called Bruno Sammartino! So my name has been Bruno ever since I can remember! My mom always called me Bruno, my sisters always called me Bruno... In fact, the only place I was ever Peter was in school – because that was my government name! So in that way I guess I grew up like two different people!" Was it this that also inspired his creativity, growing up with two separate identities? It might have helped, although in truth the young Bruno, as he now was, came from such a musical family it would have been surprising had there been any other outcome.

Music of all types filled the Hernandez household, but everyone in the family particularly loved Elvis. Not only did the tiny Bruno start picking up on all different types of musical genre, but the first song his family remember him singing was a number made famous by the King, 'All Shook Up', which Bruno began singing at the age of two. "He couldn't pronounce the words but he sang it very well," Bruno's mother, Bernie, told the *Philippine Star*, when the entire family paid a return visit to the country of her birth in 2011 to watch Bruno perform. "I think he was still in diapers. He began singing at the age of two. Singing is natural to Filipinos. I remember my father singing Spanish songs to us all the time." The whole family was musical, but due to a natural effervescence Bruno stood out. "All my kids sing, but they're shy," said Bernie. "You put them on stage and they choke, but Bruno wanted to be on stage." (In fact, his sisters were to overcome this, going on to form their own band as adults, while elder brother Eric went on to perform with his younger sibling.) "Picture a two-year old," his mother added. "Even if he couldn't pronounce the words, he would sing the beat and he was on pitch."

But her son's early start was partly down to Bernie herself: she and her brother John were at that stage performing fifties shows at the Sheraton, and when she performed she took the children along with her to scamper around backstage, absorb the atmosphere and generally grow up familiar with the smell of the greasepaint and the roar of the crowd. John was actually an Elvis impersonator, just as his little nephew was to become and there was of course also his father, Peter, with all of them performing in the same show. First he was singing Elvis songs at home, and now he was watching his uncle perform them: was there any wonder that Bruno's life took the shape it did? His early childhood could almost be seen as an apprenticeship in the light of later events – he was taught stagecraft and stage presence the way that other children are taught the alphabet. It was right there from the start. Like his sister, Uncle John noticed that Bruno stood out from a very young age: he "was always surrounded by music", he said, adding, "At every family gathering all of us would be singing, and he would be the biggest ham."

Initially, at least, it was Uncle John's work that the little Bruno found particularly intriguing, although the whole family was to prove inspirational right from the word go. "Yeah, from a very young age I remember watching the show and being completely fascinated!" Bruno later told bluesandsoul.com. "You know, my uncle would be up there playing guitar, my dad would be up there conducting the whole show, my mom would be singing out... And I'd be like 'I wanna go up there too!' So, from the moment my dad started allowing me onstage, I became a ham – and just started loving the attention! You know, I remember being four years old and just loving the fact that people were getting a kick out of my Elvis impersonation! I may not have looked like Elvis, or sounded like Elvis – but because the crowd were lapping it up, in my mind I was doing something really BIG!"

Bruno's personality had a great deal to do with his precociousness, too. Always outgoing, he was entirely at home in the world of clubs and theatre, impressing everyone else present with his energy and desire to be noticed. Everyone around him encouraged him to perform and to sing and dance, although he never had lessons in either. "He just picks up an instrument and figures it out," his father, Peter, told the *Honolulu Star Advertiser*, while his late mother told the same newspaper, "He was a natural. At age two he would lock himself in the room and do his thing over and over and over. He would come out and he would show us. When people would come over, he would point to himself [as if to say], 'Introduce me, introduce me.'" So Bruno was not only preternaturally talented from a very young age, but even then had a solid work ethic too.

Even at that age Bruno was a perfectionist, determined to get it right and learning his trade from the master himself, the King. His father would come downstairs in the middle of the night to find young Bruno watching an Elvis film on video and rehearsing the routines over and over until he got them right: "If there was a particular scene in an Elvis movie or an Elvis concert, he would watch it over and over and practise and practise imitating the moves," he said. "He could never get enough practice time."

It is possible to find footage of the little Bruno performing an Elvis impersonation and while he was quite correct in thinking that he looked and sounded nothing like the King, at the same time there is an energy and compelling quality to the performances, even in one so young. He was three when he went up on stage and by the time he was four, talk about the young musical prodigy was growing. It was actually in Japan for the opening of a Sheraton hotel that Bruno, after much pestering of his father, made his debut: "And the amazing thing was, it was something he wanted," Peter later remembered. "He always wanted to come on stage. He finally convinced me in Japan. I pulled him up on stage and he started shaking his legs and the people just went wild. I knew the novelty value was just phenomenal." It didn't hurt that at around the same time, Bernie made her precocious child an Elvis costume for Halloween: Bruno wore it out in public, started singing and promptly got inundated with people throwing money at him, making $100 in 20 minutes. A star had definitely been born.

Success is due in large part down to talent, of course, but you also have to have a certain amount of luck, and Bruno turned out to have that in spades. That Halloween night, when Bruno was strutting his infant stuff and getting an enraptured response from the crowd, there just happened to be a television crew from Hawaiian Moving Company in the vicinity. Realising that it would make sensational footage, the crew asked if they could film Bruno at the Sheraton, where his father's band, the Love Notes, were performing in the Esprit Lounge (subsequently renamed RumFire). That was that. "From that night he worked every night at age four," Bernie told the *Honolulu Star Advertiser*, although Bruno picked all his own songs "because you can't force a kid to do something he doesn't want to do".

Bruno was thriving on the attention, too. This early exposure to Elvis' music was to have a major impact on his own career. And while it might not have been pre-planned as such, what better way to excite outside attention than to have a very small child emulate the King? The real Elvis, with his sneer, his quiff and his pelvis, were about as far removed from childhood as it is possible to imagine and so it was a great talking point, at least, to have someone so young mimicking the actions of someone so much more mature (at least in years). Moreover, this was also an extended form of hero worship – of his uncle John, that is, not Elvis, about whom the very young Bruno would not have known a great deal. Many small boys hero worship a near relative and many small boys, come to that, go on to work in the family business. It's just that in Bruno's case, both the business and the hero worship were what put him on the stage. They even took him to Graceland, Elvis' estate in Memphis, where the five-year-old Bruno entertained guests, including Priscilla Presley, at a banquet. It was heady stuff.

But it wasn't all Elvis. There were plenty of other musical influences around too, many coming from his own musician father, although these other influences came from around the era when Elvis began to dominate the music scene. It was only rock'n'roll, but the entire family loved it. "Because I grew up listening to my dad who, as a fifties rock'n'roll head, loved doo-wop music," Bruno told bluesandsoul.com. "Plus doo-wop, again, is very simple! You know, I could get a guitar, play you just four chords, and sing a thousand doo-wop songs! Because they come from a time back in the day when there were no tricks! You just needed a beautiful melody, you needed a beautiful voice, and you needed to connect!"

It wasn't just his father. Bruno's mother, Bernie, was still performing as part of her husband's Love Notes doo-wop review at the then Esprit Lounge at the Sheraton Waikiki with her all-girl band, the Hi Notes, and as Bruno grew up she had a huge influence on him too. Indeed, she had a huge influence on a lot of people. She was a popular figure both inside and outside the home. "There are a lot of us girl singers out there who owe Bernadette many thanks for the opportunities she gave us," said Alison Maldonado to Honolulu Pulse after Bernie's untimely death in 2013, aged just 55, of a brain aneurism. She met Bernie in 1993 when she joined the Hi Notes as a replacement singer.

"We were all so young and inexperienced, but she saw potential in all of us. ... I loved working with her and learned a lot from watching her perform. She was the matriarch of the family, that rock that the kids definitely listened to. She knew a lot about the business, and they respected what their mama had to say," she said.

Bruno was extremely close to his mother, from his earliest days right up until the time of her death. She ruled the roost, providing security in the home and delighting all her children with her warmth and care. She was a musical influence on Bruno, but she was also a mother and homemaker, providing security for her children, and an atmosphere in which to thrive. All the children adored her, and Bruno, at a very young age, was able to show her just how much. When he was four he wrote a song called 'I Love You Mom', calling her his "favourite girl" and containing the lyrics, "My mommy helps me with my voice/ cuz a superstar singer is my first choice/My parents help me out cuz I know they love me/I just wish they buy me more toys and candy/I always brush my teeth cuz my mommy said/I do it in the morning and right before bed." It might not have been the most sophisticated of songs, but given the extreme youth of its composer, it was pretty impressive. It was an early indication of what was to come. For her part, Bernie was delighted: she had become the inspiration for her child's very first song.

And Bruno's reputation among the good people of Honolulu was continuing to grow. He was by now a professional entertainer, a habitué of the boards, with very likely a claim to be the youngest Elvis impersonator there had ever been. In 1990, by the age of four, he had featured on the cover of *MidWeek*, which also contained some choice facts about the singing toddler. "He knows he cannot get away with skipping his three-hour nap, or his mother will not allow him to go on stage," the magazine revealed. The infant Bruno is portrayed wearing the typical

Elvis regalia of sequin-covered white suit; even his hair has been tempted into a quiff. If truth be told, he looks adorable rather than fiercely sexy, but then again – he was only four. And he was sneering. He was shaking his hips. He was singing all the lyrics, even though he didn't have the faintest idea what a lot of them meant. "Performing from such a young age just got me so comfortable on stage," he told that same magazine 20 years later. "Growing up performing – that was normal for me. Everyone in my family sings, plays instruments. It's what we do." He talked again of what a big support Bernie had been to him – and indeed, it took some degree of enlightenment on the part of his mother to accept that a child so young could be making a name for himself as the King.

It did, of course, mean that Bruno was growing up extremely fast. To say that Bruno was precocious is something of an understatement. When he was still just four years old, he was interviewed by the comedian and actor Pauly Shore, who at the time had a video show on MTV. Wearing an alarming pair of brightly coloured mini-shorts, Pauly observed that Bruno had already been on NBC's *Inside Report*, CBS *Small Talk* and CNN's *World News*. "He's taking Waikiki by storm," Pauly continued. Asked to do the Elvis sneer and a few trademark moves, the infant Bruno duly obliged, before also showing himself to be a dab hand at some Michael Jackson-style strutting. The footage is still available on YouTube and shows an enchanting little boy totally lacking in nerves or self-consciousness, performing in the middle of a crowd of very amused adults. Clearly talented, the infant Bruno appears almost as amused by his watching audience as they are by him.

"There's videos and stuff of me, you can see me performing as a kid, impersonating Elvis..." he told msn.com. "I do remember that I enjoyed... that I loved just going up on stage and performing every night. As a kid I didn't know I was impersonating someone exactly but I did know that I loved getting out there on stage. As a kid my dad was a fan of a bunch of fifties rock 'n' roll; Little Richard, Elvis, Ray Charles, stuff like that. I guess I saw a couple of videos of Elvis and I just saw girls freaking out. I learned a little bit about his story, just how they were kind of scared of him because he was doing this music that wasn't supposed to be done. He was shaking his legs on TV and it was too risqué at the time... I just dug that."

Bruno was still performing every night and was becoming such a sensation that he attracted some negative attention, too. He was, after all, still little more than a toddler, and although anyone who knew him or his family, or had any knowledge of the setup, knew that Bruno was doing what Bruno was born to do, concern was expressed in some quarters that he was being exploited by his parents. This could not have been further from the truth, but even so, the concerns would not go away. And so it happened that the Hernandez family ended up in Family Court, having to explain themselves in front of a judge. The judge asked to see Bruno's act and so his father picked him up and put him on a table, where Bruno gave it his all. He was as endearing as ever, totally won over the judge and the family was vindicated. Bruno was free to tread the boards once more.

Not that his parents didn't sometimes ask themselves if they were doing the right thing: on one occasion, Bruno was so excited about going out on stage that he forgot to go to the loo beforehand, with the result that he had an embarrassing accident while wearing his jumpsuit. The audience was actually intensely amused, but feeling for the little performer, managed to smother their laughter; Bernie, meanwhile, burst into tears. Bruno, however, ever the professional, carried on as if nothing had happened. The child was a pro and wasn't going to be fazed by a little thing like that.

The interview in *MidWeek*, and the widespread publicity it attracted, turned out to be a smart career move. A year or so later, the producers of a film called *Honeymoon In Vegas* were casting around for someone to play Little Elvis, a role that would require a very young actor to sing 'Can't Help Falling In Love'. Someone, somewhere, remembered that a young child had appeared in just that guise on the cover of *MidWeek*. And so the producers contacted Bruno's family, and the whole thing snowballed from there.

It must be said, *Citizen Kane* the film was not: rather, it was just a light romp starring Nicolas Cage, James Caan and Sarah Jessica Parker and featuring a cute toddler under the name of Bruno Hernandez. When Bruno became famous 20-odd years later, his lively performance, a cute little toddler in a blue satin jumpsuit, certainly was at odds with the adult performer he would go on to become. He also featured in one of the film's "goofs": when the little Elvis is singing in the lounge, his mouth does not move with the soundtrack, and at times he turns away from the mic and his voice remains at the same volume. But it was a good-natured experience all the same.

The film garnered mixed reviews. "There is a cheerfully rising tide of goofiness in Andrew Bergman's *Honeymoon In Vegas* that is typical of his work," wrote that doyen of film critics, the late Roger Ebert, in the *Chicago Sun-Times*. "This is the writer-director of *The Freshman*, in which the members of a gourmet diners' club proposed to eat a threatened species of lizard, and so perhaps we should not be surprised this time when the hero finds himself unexpectedly part of a team of skydiving Elvis impersonators. What is surprising is how, by that point in the film, it seems more or less logical."

Bruno himself got a mention (albeit not by name) in another review. "Las Vegas is always gaudy and photogenic, but Mr. Bergman's vision is something new," wrote Vincent Canby in the *New York Times*. "It's a folksy Fellini daydream in which the Elvis Presleys come in all sizes, ages, shapes and colours. As Elvis music drenches the soundtrack, the King's would-be lookalikes line up at the reservations desk, sidle through the gaming rooms and appear on stage at the supper club, including one who is five years old. The motley crowd of Elvises is not only funny in itself, but it also defines the engagingly lunatic environment in which so many commonplace things can go so wildly wrong."

Owen Gleiberman, in *Entertainment Weekly*, however, was considerably less impressed. "I really, really wanted to like *Honeymoon In Vegas*, the sweet-'n'-zany new comedy about a guy, a gal, a gangster, and a planeload of skydiving Elvis impersonators," he began. "I mean, how could a movie featuring the Flying Elvises be anything less than... entertaining? Here's how. In *Honeymoon In Vegas*, Nicolas Cage plays an earnest, mother-whipped nebbish, and Sarah Jessica Parker – who's like Madonna as a Vassar lit major – is his improbably sexy schoolteacher girlfriend. The two arrive in Vegas, where Cage, after much arm-twisting, has agreed to tie the knot. That's when they're spotted by James Caan, a professional gambler and thug who thinks the willowy Parker is the spitting image of his dead wife. Smitten, he tricks Cage into joining a rigged poker game and bilks him out of $60,000. Then he offers him a deal: Forget the money and give me your fiancée for the weekend." There was more along the same lines, but the message was clear – he was not impressed.

Critics overall were similarly divided along these lines, but it was Bruno's first experience of film making and his first taste of life in the mainstream entertainment industry, although it was to be another two decades before he made it on his own.

By now, his musical range was broadening: Jimi Hendrix was becoming an inspiration, as were the likes of Frank Sinatra and the Rat Pack, who impressed the young Bruno with their immaculately sharp style, and above all by Michael Jackson, whose perfectionism was to have a major impact on Bruno's adult career.

Nor was he just singing, he was learning to play instruments, eventually mastering drums, keyboard, bass and guitar. All of the elements of his later life were beginning to fall into place.

And so, by the end of the eighties, Bruno was already a seasoned performer, could hold his own on stage against adult singers, and had appeared in a film — all by the age of six. Performing had become a passion, and it was influencing every area of his life, including even what he was looking for in a woman. Bruno was a little young to start thinking about relationships, but he did notice the showgirls, with their glamorous outfits, that surrounded him: "I was like, 'These girls don't look like the girls I go to school with,'" he said in a highly personal and revealing interview with *Rolling Stone*. Indeed, performing sure beat the heck out of schoolwork: "I would look forward to getting out of school," Bruno went on. "Just looking at the clock, waiting for it to hit 2.15." This period went on until he was about 11 years old, with Bruno the star amongst his classmates, but desperate to get out of school, up on stage and doing his stuff with the rest of the family. It seemed that nothing could go wrong.

The young Bruno was certainly indulged by his parents, as when he decided he was interested in DIY. "I told my mum and dad I really want this tool box when I was really young and they bought it for me for Christmas," he told *The Sun*. "Now that I think about it, I was really young to have a real tool set. It had a saw, a hammer and real nails. I must have put 100 nails in our dinner table." Money was no object. He could have whatever he liked.

It was a golden time, but it was not to last. Bruno's father, Peter, had been doing very well financially: at one stage he had seven Cadillacs while the family home in Kahala was enormous. Bruno himself had a huge bedroom housing miniature drum kits, pianos and guitars. But all was not well. Peter and Bernie's marriage was coming under great strain and began to crumble, and if the marriage couldn't survive, then the band wouldn't either. Peter had a range of businesses (including one selling Elvis memorabilia), but they, too, began to go wrong. What had been a gilded existence was turning sour and for all his youthful precocity, Bruno began to experience the first of a series of setbacks, although in some ways this might have been the making of him. Up until now success had come very easily, but now he was having to learn how to cope when life doesn't go according to plan. That was an essential talent to learn: show business is one of the most precarious careers on the planet and anyone entering into it has to be aware that it could all vanish tomorrow – and that sometimes it's essential to fight back.

Bruno was about to go through this. He was about to see his parents' marriage break up, his show-business career disappear and a big change in family circumstances, which saw him moving from a big, comfortable home to considerably more rickety surroundings. Life as he knew it was about to change completely. And he wouldn't enjoy anything like the success he'd had to date for the best part of 16 years.

Chapter 3

The Lean Years

As the young Bruno began to grow up, initially, at least, it seemed as if matters were going to go OK. By the age of six he had also managed an appearance on *The Arsenio Hall Show*, and he was now also singing imitations of Frankie Lymon and Little Anthony, a really excellent training, did he but know it, for what was to lie ahead later in life. Bruno has sometimes seemed embarrassed as an adult that he did so many impersonations as a child and sang so many other people's music, but the truth is that it was a very good way to learn his trade. But it was not to last. The break-up of his parents' marriage and a dip in his father's business interests meant that, at a very young age, Bruno was to learn that you can lose everything almost overnight. Aged 11, Bruno and his father had to move to what he later called "the slums of Hawaii", a massive shift from what had been a previously wealthy and cushioned lifestyle. The young Bruno was in a state of shock, and for some time life became very difficult indeed. But setbacks can make you stronger and it could well have been this early disadvantage that gave Bruno the impetus to succeed.

It certainly didn't feel like that at the time. The move also heralded a change of school. At his old school Bruno had been something of a star but that was not the case here and he began to be bullied, which caused deep scars that would endure well into his later life. For some reason he began to be called Peter Pan Hyma Dingler, the first part, presumably, because he looked so young, although the second part remains a mystery. "Even the nerds were calling me that!" he said years later in an interview with *Rolling Stone*, and although he was laughing about it, it was clear that it had caused terrible hurt. "Oh, man it was rough. I didn't even want to go to school. But then the guys that called me that became my good friends."

Part of the problem was that he was vulnerable: he looked so young and he was the new kid on the block, always a difficult position to be in when there's an extended crowd around. Also, not to put too fine a point on it, Bruno was short. As an adult, he stands at 5′ 5″ which has made no difference whatsoever either in his career or when it comes to his love life, but back then, as the other kids started to grow, it marked him out. He was isolated, small and had gone from a wealthy background to a much more modest situation. It was not a happy time.

Elsewhere it seemed that matters were going from bad to worse. Bruno's father was very badly off by now but, determined that he would do what he could to try to revive his son's career, he took what was left of his Elvis memorabilia to a flea market and sold it all for $125. Bruno then saw a Fender guitar on sale for $115 – and his father bought it for him. "It was literally all the money he had," Bruno told *Rolling Stone*. But it was still to be a long time before Peter saw any return on that investment – Bruno was still nowhere near the heights that he had scaled while he was still so young. And money was getting tighter all the time. "We were so poor we used to take Top Ramen noodles and put some ragu on it and call it spaghetti," he tweeted in February 2012 (although he did later say, "Now I eat diamonds"). It was becoming a somewhat desolate situation. The only consolation was the depth of the bond between Bruno and his father, and indeed, the rest of the family. The parents might have divorced, but the siblings continued to be extremely close, of which more anon.

But this was an exceptionally unhappy period of Bruno's life. And it marked him, for good. For better or worse, no one ever forgets an unhappy childhood and Bruno was now in a situation where he was having a bad time at school, his parents were divorced, there was no money and he'd lost the career he'd had as a child. But as he was later to confess himself, in a strange way, this had its own advantages, too. To succeed in a career as unstable as show business requires plenty of ambition and drive and that is, in many cases, what an unhappy childhood produces. There is always the determination to prove the naysayers wrong, to show that you can make something of your life after all. Countless other household names had very difficult times in the past (Tom Cruise, who had a chaotic childhood, was also bullied) and it is very possible that going through this down phase pushed Bruno onwards in the future. Certainly, apart from the cocaine episode in Vegas, Bruno appreciated success when it finally arrived. He knew what it was like to go through the tough times – it made him appreciate the good times all the more.

Bruno was a student at President Theodore Roosevelt High School throughout his teen years, a public co-ed school located in Honolulu. Coincidentally, the school itself, while not connected to the entertainment industry per se, appeared as the backdrop in several movie and television productions due to its distinctive appearance, with a domed bell tower and long building constructed in the Spanish mission architectural style. It was an attractive place: right next to the bell tower is a sculpture by Mark Watson, entitled *Ho'okahi (To Make As One)*. With a strong musical tradition, Bruno was not its only famous son:

other singers to have attended the school were Alfred Apaka and Yvonne Elliman, while other notable alumni included congressman Thomas Gill, Olympian wrestler Clarissa Chun and baseball player Mike Lum.

No one was claiming that Bruno was the world's most academic student, however. All he cared about really was making music – and, increasingly, girls. Bruno's charm in part was due to his laid back Hawaiian background, but also the sheer force of his personality, and women were to find him very attractive from a very young age. Even when he was a struggling musician, with seemingly no prospects of making it anywhere, of which more anon, there was never any shortage of female attention. And it started when he was very young. The only problem, though, was that the taunting continued, for it didn't help Bruno in the eyes of some of his male counterparts that he was increasingly popular with the girls.

After a time, however, things began to look up. The bullying stopped and Bruno found himself popular; he was also continuing to catch the eye of the girls even more than he had done previously. That baby face was turning into something else: a sharply chiselled profile in which cheekbones were beginning to emerge from strongly defined bone structure. He was also a bit of a dandy: "I always rocked an afro in high school," he once told rap-up.com. It did no harm to Bruno's growing popularity at all. Indeed, that early awareness of his image was another facet to his personality that would stand him in good stead as an adult. When Bruno burst on to the scene, it was with an extremely sharp image. From very early on, Bruno understood the importance of appearance. It was just that here he was on a domestic stage – the wider audience was still some years ahead.

At the same time, he was still making music: he got together with high-school friends Joey Kaalekahi, Dwayne Andres and Reid Kobashigawa to form a group called The School Boys. At

14, Bruno was the youngest of the quartet, as Reid was 16, Joey 17 and Dwayne 18, but his talent marked him apart even then. The boys got together after Joey and Dwayne were working out some vocals with Reid at around the time that Bruno joined the school and they asked the newcomer to join. Bruno was delighted to do so. Indeed, for a time it seemed as if his future lay in a boy band rather than as a solo singer and the boys even discussed taking on a fifth member (the requirements were that he should be 18 or younger, fun, serious about a career in music and willing to sing both oldies and contemporary material. Oh, and he should also have a car). In the event Peter Isaia also sang with the group, although history does not record whether he had the required vehicle. Peter also went on to have a career in the music industry, as did Dwayne, a music producer and songwriter, who became known as Drehz. It was yet another formative experience that would shape Bruno for the future and it also marked a total end to the bullying. It was official: Bruno was now a talented musician and popular with the girls.

As Bruno himself had been doing up until then, the School Boys performed music by other artists, teaching themselves a variety of styles as they went along. Indeed, the group would perform music by the Isley Brothers and the Temptations, extending Bruno's repertoire. Offstage, they were experimenting with more contemporary music, an early experiment on Bruno's part with creating his own music, something else that would stand him in good stead during the period when he thought his solo career would have to go on hold while he created music for other people in the early days of the Smeezingtons, the singers/writers/producers with whom Bruno was to make his name.

At the same time, his father, Peter, was playing with the Love Notes again and was teaching him to play Ventures, Chuck Berry and Carlos Santana on his guitar. Bruno would occasionally perform with his father's band, performing songs such as 'My

Girl', while carrying on at school, and the School Boys were also sometimes up on the stage with the Love Notes after Bruno had asked his father if they could audition. It was not a given that they would be allowed to perform – they had to prove themselves before they were allowed on stage. In the event, however, the School Boys were to prove a great success.

They had a lot of fun, as befits young boys of their age finding their feet in the world. The *Honolulu Star* actually published a feature on the boys way back in 2000, which related how two girls, Rene Uchida and Jebelyn Carino, were on their way to the Jack In The Box nightclub when they realised four young men were eyeing them up. Quite suddenly, one of them shouted, "We want to sing for you." The next moment, to the girls' great bemusement, the School Boys (for it was they) were serenading them, Bruno putting his heart into it all. "No one ever did that before. Never," Uchida told the paper with commendable understatement.

Bruno (still known as Bruno Fernandez back then) took up the tale. "We had a great show that night and we were ready for anything," he said. "We saw those two girls and something had to happen."

Over to Dwayne: "When Reid went out [of the car] we all had to follow," he said. "I think they were shocked we could sing but now it's one of those romantic things you'll always remember." If it was a novel way of expanding their fanbase, it certainly worked: the girls went on to watch them perform on stage several times. Photos still exist from that time: they show four bright-faced boys gleaming with excitement, beams spread across their faces. They featured the look of the time: white T-shirts, oversized jeans hanging low on the hips and expensive trainers. Joey and Reid favoured baseball caps, Bruno a chain around his neck. And with that attitude, was it any wonder Bruno was popular with the girls? He was later to claim that his singing voice was a direct result of his teenage years spent serenading the ladies – it certainly got him noticed and increasingly popular.

It was all teaching him his trade. At home, after school, privately, professionally – absolutely everywhere there was music. "Growing up in the showbiz world, I looked up to those guys," he told *Playboy*. "Frank Sinatra and of course Elvis Presley. My dad was into the fifties doo-wop era. If you look at those groups, or at James Brown, Jackie Wilson and the Temptations in the sixties, you'll see you had to be sharp onstage." Jimi Hendrix was also a huge influence: "I think he's the greatest guitar player in the world, and I would want to see him do his thing in person. He's the reason I picked up a guitar in the first place," he said when asked about a dream collaboration.

Until his mid-teens, however, Bruno's musical success had always been based on other people – imitating Elvis and more latterly Michael Jackson, right down to the famous moonwalk, something that he still does on stage, although not that often. "Just because I can moonwalk," he told *Rolling Stone*, "doesn't mean I should moonwalk." Apart from his act with the School Boys, however, he hadn't actually done a great deal himself, as Bruno Mars. All that changed in his sophomore year during a pep rally. Bruno suddenly leaped on to the stage and gave a rendition of Ginuwine's 'Pony': while the teachers were livid that he had used the word "horny", the girls all went wild. That was a seminal moment for Bruno: it changed everything, not only in the way that he was perceived but what he felt about himself. "After that, I walked around the halls like I was Sinatra," he told *Rolling Stone*. "I was like, 'OK, I'm not just an impersonator. I can also impersonate Genuwine!'" But it was more than that and he knew it. Bruno had not only talent but charisma, stage presence and an ability to wow the ladies. It was one day going to be a mix that would take him far.

And the girls continued to love it. Bruno himself is very coy about when his relationships with women started properly, but it is rumoured that it was around now, at about the age of 16. Although he was still relatively young, it is thought that he was dating a singer in her early twenties, a relationship he concealed from his parents, especially his mother, knowing that she would disapprove. Bruno himself refuses to talk about it – "My mother and father taught me that a gentleman doesn't kiss and tell" – but the fact is that even at that young age, he was already very attractive to women. Again, much has been written about his height, or lack of it, but again, it was irrelevant. And this attractiveness to women was not just something that was personally pleasing for Bruno, but a crucial element of his show-business career. The vast majority of performers need sex appeal in order to broaden their appeal as widely as possible. Bruno was already there.

That light-bulb moment in high school began to transfer itself into a modicum of professional success. He was back on stage professionally, opening the act for a big magic show, for which he got $75 a pop, and he was back impersonating Michael Jackson again, as well. Now Bruno was beginning to think of the longer term: the end of his high-school days was approaching and he was beginning to think about going professional. Why not? Music had been his greatest interest since the days that he was a toddler and both parents were in the industry. In the event, in fact, about half the Fernandez children were to end up in the music industry.

Back at school, however, it was safe to say that Bruno was no academic. With his music after school and in the evening taking precedence over just about anything else, he was never going to be a Grade A student, and indeed he was not. But he was convinced, more and more, that music was to be his future and in later years he was to credit the environment he grew up in for making him the musician he became. It was not just that his immediate family was very musical: the very society in which he lived was musical. It was part of everyday life.

"Yeah, everyone in Hawaii is really laid-back and happy and content with life – because everyone knows the BEACH is right outside!" he told *Blues And Soul*. "And so music is just in the AIR, basically! It's just everywhere you GO! You know, there's always someone around with a guitar who's ready to SING! Like you see these big, 200-pound Hawaiian guys singing in the sweetest voices ever! I mean, you simply cannot go to a barbecue without someone playing the guitar and singing!"

It was bound to rub off. While he might still have been some way away from being famous, Bruno was being encouraged simply by basking in his surroundings. In the laid-back beach culture in which he lived, making music was as natural as eating and breathing. And there was still a tradition of what might be called a troubador – people singing as a response to everything they came across in life. Bruno was right about the big men with the sweet voices, too: possibly the most famous Hawaiian singer before Bruno himself was the late Israel Kamakawiwo'ole, a giant of a man with a mellifluous voice that could melt granite. Bruno came from the same culture and it was having the same effect on him.

"And so I guess that's how I became how I am - just ready to sing and play at any point!" he went on. "I mean, reggae is huge out there! And if you ever listen to Hawaiian music you'll hear that, even if you can't understand Hawaiian, the melody is incredible! It's just memorable, classic melody that, once you hear it, you'll never forget!... So I guess growing up there did in turn play a big part in helping me to write songs like that – with melodies that stick!"

High school really was nearing an end now. Bruno was as popular with the girls as ever and so when it came time to go to the prom, there was no shortage of willing partners for him to escort. There are still pictures online of the young Bruno off to the prom: wearing a dinner jacket and an enormous afro, he had by now grown into his looks. Other pictures that circulated show him with a pretty partner; Bruno has always said that he was never a player, but he was clearly becoming a very attractive man. But other preoccupations were beginning to make themselves felt. What was Bruno going to do with his future? Was his life to remain in Hawaii or should he seek his fortunes elsewhere? And should he really try to make his way in show business? Now, of course, the answer seems obvious – his entire life to date would seem to be a preparation for the life that Bruno was to have. But show business is a notoriously difficult arena in which to forge a career and indeed, there were going to be quite a few false starts before Bruno really got going. But at the same time, there was really no obvious alternative and nothing else that Bruno particularly wanted to do. And so the stage was set. Bruno was going to take the biggest gamble of his life.

Chapter 4

LA Confidential

Bruno graduated – just – in 2003, with one thing on his mind: to become a musician. All that childhood experience had paid off: he was clearly a very talented musician, although he was not, as yet, a songwriter. Circumstances were to propel him to become one, although that was still in the future.

And so, he sent a demo tape to one of his sisters, who was now living in Los Angeles and working as a handbag designer. She played it for Mike Lynn, then a music executive at Dr Dre's Aftermath Entertainment, and although Bruno later claimed that he'd sounded like a chipmunk, Lynn clearly heard something, because Bruno was summoned to LA in order to meet music industry executives, press the flesh and see where life took him. Dr Dre, born Andre Romelle Young, was a record producer, rapper and entrepreneur, who had first found fame with the World Class Wreckin' Cru and was now a serious mover and shaker in the record industry. Was he to be the man who discovered Bruno? Not exactly. But his interest, or rather, that of one of his executives, was enough to convince Bruno and his family that there was a real chance he would find fame and success in music, and so it was that he took a chance.

Initially Bruno lived with his sister – a number of family members had already made the move over there. Hawaii might have been beautiful, but he had to be at the centre of the action if he wanted to get anywhere. And so the first step in Bruno's journey from small-time small-town entertainer had been taken – but it was going to be a long hard slog before Bruno finally found himself where he really wanted to be.

Nonetheless, the break had been made – Bruno had left Hawaii and moved to the centre of the music industry. "I accomplished a lot in Hawaii as an entertainer, but never really dabbled in original music," he told rap-up.com, in an interview from 2010, which revealed that he missed the more laid-back side of Hawaiian life. "I was like a circus freak – I used to sing songs, I used to open up for a Las Vegas-style magic show. I'd sing songs for all the tourists. It was always cover songs – everything from Chuck Berry to Usher. Then I got fed up, like I'm singing songs to a bunch of tourists that don't even speak English. I felt like I could do more. I do miss Hawaii though. People over there are real content and satisfied with just being on an island, having kids a very young age. It's not like you're trying to be an actor or trying to be a musician with millions of other people, and it's just hustle, hustle, hustle." There spoke the voice of disillusionment. Bruno was to come to love his life in Los Angeles, but to begin with, at least, it was quite a culture shock. And making it in the music business was going to prove much, much harder than he had thought.

There was certainly going to be plenty of disappointment in store. Bruno was 17 when he got to LA and 18 when, at first, it seemed he had a huge stroke of luck – he was signed up very quickly by the record label Universal Motown. At first, it looked like he'd got it made. He and his brother Eric had formed a band called Sex Panther alongside a friend called Jeff Bhasker, a producer who went on to work alongside Kanye. Bruno had met Jeff through Mike Lynn, and they would play to small crowds along Ventura Boulevard at small-scale bars dotted around the area. They would play covers of any requests the punters asked for, which at least supplied some income, before Jeff went off to work with Kanye as a keyboard player. The band broke up, but at least Bruno had his Motown contract. Or so he thought.

Although Bruno had been spending a good deal of time in the studio, for some reason his sound just wasn't coming together. The trouble was that no one seemed to know what to do with him and so barely a year after signing, and without any major release, major news or major breakthrough, the label dropped him. To a young man on the cusp of a career, it was a shattering development – although in the longer term, it would turn out to have been for the best.

This was to be the first of a number of major disappointments. Bruno was shell shocked, or as he put it, his heart dropped out. He went extremely quickly from promising new hopeful to a man with a great future behind him. And apart from anything else, there was the loss of face. His friends and family all knew he seemed to be on the verge of a great new career – and then, just like that, it was gone. The temptation to move home was stronger than it had ever been, not least because Bruno had not really acclimatised to LA, but he knew at the back of his mind this would be a bad mistake. It would have been throwing away all chance of success, no matter what disappointments he had had to cope with, and something told him he would get another chance. "If I had moved back to Hawaii, I felt I never would have made it back up here," he told friends. "I would have been at the Polynesian Review with a ukulele and an aloha shirt, probably singing Elvis tunes. Again." But he had been very, very disappointed. And it was to take years before he found his niche.

Years later, after success had finally arrived (and it took its time in coming), Bruno was able to reflect on it, although the wounds went very deep at the time. In some ways, he blamed himself, while admitting that it gave him just the jolt he needed. "I wasn't ready for it," he told *Billboard* magazine in 2011. "I did nothing. And the lesson was – why are you waiting for someone to come and write a song with you? You know how to play the freakin' guitar. Do it on your own."

But that did not happen immediately, and at any rate, Bruno had been very bruised by the experience. He opened up about it to Piers Morgan on national television in 2012 and it was clear that it had hurt him deeply at the time. "It was taking a step back," he said. "I used to be able to walk into a room and say, 'Hey, I'm Bruno Mars, I'm signed with Motown Records.' Now I have to say, 'I got dropped from Motown Records.' You lose leverage. You lose people believing in you because, then, (they say) 'Why didn't it work?'

"It was like this... 'Hey, we don't want you any more'. And you know what? It's not Motown's fault. I was too young. I didn't know what it was like. I knew I could sing... but there's so much more I had to learn. I didn't come from the recording background. I came from doing live shows and performing with bands and that was my craft. I didn't know what it took to become... to record and be a recording artist. Establish who you are... I don't know if anyone knows who they are at 18 years old. I might have cried. I might have shed some tears. You definitely have those nights where you feel a little insecure, but I didn't want to give up. My goal was, 'I'm not going to go back home. I'm not going back to Hawaii and face my friends and my family saying it didn't pan out. I've got to do something.' I think I grew. I grew as an artist. I grew as a writer. I wrote songs every day. I started producing. And you know, practice is what you need."

It was a laudable decision not to blame Motown and accept

that actually, despite having a vast wealth of experience behind him, far more than most would-be stars of his age, Bruno had to learn his trade. But those interviews did not sum up the full story of what would turn out to be some pretty desperate years. Bruno had already experienced setbacks as a child when his parents split up and his father had business difficulties; now it was going to get even worse. And there were all sorts of problems Bruno had not been expecting, not least surrounding whatever race he may or may not be. In actual fact, his parentage stemmed from all over the world, but at that stage, still called Bruno Fernandez, no one quite knew who he really was and what category, either of race or indeed music, they should slot him in to. Was he black, Asian, Spanish or what exactly? In actual fact, he was a mixture of all these and more, but for a music industry that likes to slot its performers into boxes, this ambiguity really didn't help. It was because of what happened at this stage of his life that Bruno finally decided to change his surname, as it was leading to too much confusion as it was.

"Your last name's Hernandez, maybe you should do this Latin music, this Spanish music…. Enrique's so hot right now," was how he put it to *GQ* in later years, describing the reaction of record-label bosses when he met them for the first time. He wanted to avoid being stereotyped, and so the only way to do it was to choose a name that couldn't be associated with any country or type of music in the world. Or as Bruno himself somewhat cornily put it, "I felt like I didn't have pizzazz and a lot of girls say I'm out of this world, so I was like, I guess I'm from Mars."

Not that changing his name seemed to do him a great deal of good. Unwilling to take a risk, not sure how to market him and displaying a colossal lack of imagination, one record company after another turned him down. It was extraordinarily disheartening: all that talent fizzing around and no proper outlet for it. On top of everything else, Bruno's money was beginning to run out. It had been a long time since the wealth of his early childhood and Bruno needed to earn an income, but how? If no one wanted to employ him as a musician, what was he going to do?

And, for that matter, how was he going to carry on making music at all if he didn't have the wherewithal to do so? Because matters got so bad that to raise some money he at one point had to get rid of the lot. "At my lowest point I had to sell all my instruments, because I couldn't pay my house any more and my phone got disconnected," he told a Dutch magazine. "Having a distance from your guitar and drum is the most terrible thing that could happen as a musician." But it was that or get kicked out on to the streets: Bruno was existing on practically nothing. Meanwhile the record companies continued to ignore him. Matters were rapidly going from bad to worse.

In the event Bruno got so desperate that he found a job selling insurance, which he turned out to be pretty good at, although he hated it and wanted to return to his musical career. He also had a short-term stint as a DJ, for which he was paid $75 cash down per session, something else that didn't last long when it became apparent Bruno had no idea how to DJ. "I couldn't pay rent," he told *Entertainment Weekly*. "I'd always been a working musician in Hawaii and never had problems paying rent. And then it's like, 'Now I'm in LA and my phone's getting shut off.' That's when reality hit. I started DJing. It was something silly. I told this person I could DJ because they said they could pay me $75 cash under the table. I didn't know how to DJ. I lost that job pretty quick."

But he was showing persistence, that was for sure. There is no industry harder to break into and make a success of than the entertainment industry and the vast majority of performers who do make the breakthrough have to fight every inch of the way. Bruno was turning out to be one of those. Those early setbacks, the bullying at school, the hard times in his father's business, had all helped to create an inner steel that was now standing him in very good stead. To give up at that stage would have been easy but disastrous – it would have meant that Bruno would now still be selling insurance, rather than producing all the hits he has done to date. But it was not easy to keep the faith.

"There was a lot of rejection," he told *Billboard* magazine years later. "A lot of other labels saying, 'You don't know who the hell you are. You're doing all this reggae, R&B, rock stuff. How the hell do we market that? Are you pop? Are you urban?'" It was remarkable that he managed to keep going at all with so very little encouragement, but deep down Bruno believed in himself. However, he had to change his approach in some way – and eventually he did.

The problem, not that anyone realised it at the time, was that Bruno was still using other people's material. Given that he'd started out as an impersonator and developed his talent by singing songs made famous by others, despite all that early musical prowess and despite the fact that he could play a range of musical instruments, it had never actually occurred to him that he could write music for himself. It hadn't occurred to anyone else either, which is why, by a stroke of great good luck, Bruno came to the attention of Brandon Creed. Brandon, now manager of the Creed Company, was at the time A&R executive at Epic and he finally saw something that no one else had. In later years he was to admit he "wasn't 100 per cent sure the artist thing was going to be a go", but he saw enough to give Bruno one of the best pieces of career advice he was ever to receive, namely to start writing music himself. Bruno was initially staggered, but once he'd taken it on board, he began to like the idea.

"Brandon was always saying, 'You need a story. You need to be in the studio writing for people,'" he told *Billboard*. "At the time I was like, 'You're crazy. I'm amazing!' But he was absolutely right. Working and interacting with other artists and being so involved with the business aspect; understanding A&R, understanding radio, understanding music videos meant that when it came to my time, I'd seen how it goes."

It was to prove the making of him – and Brandon, too. Increasingly convinced that there was something special about Bruno, Brandon decided to put his money where his mouth was and join forces with the man who would one day become a global superstar. He quit his job at A&R and became Bruno's manager. Now, at last, Bruno had the guidance of someone a little bit older, who already knew the entertainment industry, and who he could bounce ideas back on. And he was the perfect choice. Brandon had started his career at Arista Records, moving to J Records, where he worked with the likes of Pearl Jam, Dido and Santana, mainly as product manager. It was when he moved to Epic that he became involved in A&R: he worked with the likes of Jennifer Lopez and Brandy and was behind the signing of Jasmine V and Sean Kingston. Meeting him was the start of a big change in Bruno's luck.

Matters improved slightly in other ways, too. In 2005, Bruno met Steve Lindsey and Cameron Strang at Westside Independent through his early contact Mike Lynn, who very much took him under their wing. Steve was a very experienced record producer, songwriter, music publisher and music industry executive, who had worked with some of the most famous artists in the business, including Elton John, Luther Vandross, Leonard Cohen and others too numerous to mention, and it was he who taught Dr Dre piano and music theory for four years. In 2004, he established Westside Independent publishing with Cameron and another of their protégés was Brody Brown, with whom Bruno was later to work. It was Steve who really began to teach Bruno how to write music: as his friend Jeff Bhasker, who also worked with Lindsey, told *American Entertainment*: "He'd mentor us, and kind of give us lectures as to what a hit pop song is, because you can have talent and music ability, but understanding what makes a hit pop song is a whole other discipline."

Indeed, he was a hard taskmaster. At the 2013 ASCAP Expo, a musician wrote about what she had learnt from Lindsey at the conference: "[Steve Lindsey] told us the importance of knowing at least three hours of cover material. His point was, it is difficult to be a great songwriter without extensively studying great music on a daily basis. He told us that he held Bruno Mars back for five years while they learned an extensive catalogue of hit music."

Clearly, it was going to be a hard slog. Initially the record labels hadn't known what to do with Bruno as a singer: now they didn't know what to do with him as a songwriter. But Bruno had a real goal to work towards now, and as he recounted it later, it all went into making him into the musician he was going to become. "Those days when I was dropped and was shopping some songs that we'd written to different labels and they were saying it was too unorthodox..." he told the *Independent* newspaper. "It all happens for a reason and it's all part of my story. Learn the hard way that you gotta know who you are, and know what you want, and know what you want to sound like, and walk into a label saying, 'This is me, take it or leave it.'" It was certainly toughening him up in a way that was to serve him well. But now he had Brandon as his backup, someone to encourage him. Bruno knew that for all his travails, people with a great deal of experience and knowledge of the industry knew that he had what it takes. To put it at its most basic – Bruno wasn't alone any more.

Chapter 5

The Smeezingtons

It was downtown LA, and two young men were feeling pretty desperate. They had been knocking around the edges of the music industry for some time now, with varying degrees of lack of success: Bruno had been signed and dropped by Motown and was feeling like giving up. Philip Lawrence knew how he felt. The two had a great deal in common: six years older than Bruno, Philip was a would-be singer/songwriter/producer, who was also in town. Like Bruno, Philip came from an extremely musical family from a small town called Evansville in Indiana and like Bruno he had been surrounded by music all his life. He had even been another child performer, up on stage pretty much as a toddler, and well used to the show-business industry from very early childhood. Like Bruno, it had seemed the obvious area in which to try to carve out a path for himself and like Bruno, it hadn't gone according to plan.

"I come from a real music family," he told thenext2shine.com. "My mother was the choir director of my gospel choir. Like, 90 per cent of the people in my family are singers. So I knew at a very young age – I think the first time I was on stage I was like four years old. I've been performing and I have had music in my life from a very young age. My dad was a DJ in the seventies so I always had crates and crates of albums lying around the house. So at any given time we could be listening to some Stevie Wonder all the way to the Eagles, to Led Zeppelin, Ohio Players, you name it and it was in our living room."

It was hardly surprising that the two of them were going to get on so well when they eventually met. So far, so much in common, but that wasn't all. Both were horribly short of money and both had to take on jobs they hated to make ends meet: Philip had worked for Disney for the best part of seven years doing, among much else, voiceovers as Sebastian in *The Little Mermaid* and dressing as Simba from *The Lion King*, which wasn't so bad, but much, much worse were his occasional stints in telesales. Again, like Bruno in his insurance days, he was forced to work in an area he hated, but had to do so just to get some food on the table and to pay the rent. Could he take much more of this? Probably not.

As with Bruno, it was the lack of money that was the biggest problem and out in Los Angeles, where appearance counts for so much, it was no joke spending your days stony broke. Not only did it make day-to-day life difficult, but it actually limited your possibilities, as Bruno had discovered when he had to sell his musical instruments. It was a vicious circle: you needed money to prosper but if you weren't prospering, then you had no money. What was a person to do? Indeed, Philip was so short of money that when Keith Harris, drummer for the Black Eyed Peas as well as a music producer and a mutual friend of both Bruno and Philip, suggested the duo should meet, it almost didn't take place as Philip couldn't afford it. Fortunately he was talked around, and into a meeting that would change both their lives.

In later years, when everyone involved was rolling in loot, the fact that this crucial meeting was nearly abandoned just for the lack of a few bucks was treated with amusement by Bruno and Philip, but it was most certainly no laughing matter at the time. "One day he [Keith] just called me up and said 'Hey man I got this kid who is super talented, he is signed to such-and-such label but I think he's looking to get in a new situation,'" Philip told thenext2shine.com, on one of the many occasions when he recalled how it all came about. Bruno was by this time having a little more luck in his own career and at least managing to attract a little attention from record bosses, although he was still finding it very difficult to make that final breakthrough. "'We're doing some great work but you know he could use a writer to kind of help him get his ideas out.' I could remember at the time I was beyond broke. I was living in LA and didn't have a car and for years I was taking public transportation. So it was going to cost me my last five dollars to get to the studio. I was like 'Yo Keith is he really good man. Please tell me he is.' But me and Bruno hit it off and that first session was the first time either of us had fully written, recorded, and produced a song in one night. From that point on, we haven't stopped working together."

It was a musical marriage made in heaven, in fact, working on every possible level, both personally and professionally. For a start, the two men liked one another and got on extremely well. Personal chemistry at that stage was crucial: given that both had been feeling pretty hopeless, they needed each other to provide professional energy, to give them that last push to get ahead. It certainly helped that they had so much in common and could relate to each other's experience of the massive difficulties involved in getting ahead in the music business, but it was an immediate sense of shared camaraderie that really helped them hit it off.

And so they started to write. Bruno was still relatively new to this aspect of the business, but he was turning out to be pretty good at it and now that he had someone to write with, his creative juices were really beginning to flow. Not that success came at once: Bruno and Philip had previously both had a good deal of experience being rejected as solo artists and now they were getting the same thing as a duo. Not that Bruno had given up on the dream of making it as a solo singer: when his big breakthrough finally came, many people assumed that he was a songwriter embarking on some kind of vanity project, whereas in fact the ambition to go it alone as a singer had been part of the plan all along. Indeed, in the very early days, the work he and Philip were doing was indeed designed to launch him as a singer. Right at the beginning, it hadn't occurred to them to write for anyone else.

It was around this time that Philip introduced Bruno to the person who was one day going to be his A&R manager at Atlantic records, Aaron Bay-Schuck. Aaron had entered the music business in 2003, straight out of university, and was at Atlantic by the time the two men met. Aaron saw Bruno's potential right away, but the record label took some time to be convinced. "It was a long process," Aaron told Hitquarters in 2010, the year of Bruno's breakthrough. "His songwriting partner Philip Lawrence first introduced me to him in 2006. The first time Bruno played the guitar and sang a couple of the songs he had written for himself I was blown away. I wanted to sign him immediately but it took a few years to get Atlantic excited about him. I used him as a songwriter and producer for all of those years but as an artist it took some time to get everyone to see our vision."

Crucially, Aaron knew from the start that Bruno would one day want to go it alone. "Bruno made it clear from the beginning that being an artist was always his biggest goal, but that he was also willing to write and produce and do anything that it took to be recognised as an artist," Aaron continued. "I wanted to sign him instantly but it was a long-term process. He had to spend a lot of time improving his songwriting and trying to find out exactly who he wanted to be as an artist. If Atlantic had let me sign him four years ago who knows if the outcome would have been the same. He always had the talent, but he definitely went through some self-discovery over the past few years that contributed in a big way to his recent success."

In hindsight, of course, it was all to work out well, but no one knew that back in the day. For all the hard work and recognition from some individual quarters, they weren't getting anywhere. And this time round, they really did start to despair. Most artists retain some insecurity about the true extent of their ability – they wouldn't be human if they didn't – and in the face of so much rejection, they really did come very close to giving up. Would they ever be taken up by anyone? At times it seemed not. "He and I were writing songs for him as a solo artist, then would go to labels and get no's everywhere," Philip told *American Songwriter*. "Finally it got to be really desperate because we started thinking we weren't as good as we thought we were. We were toying with the idea of him moving back to Hawaii, and I was going to move back to Florida to go work at Disney World (where I was working before coming to LA)."

The pair came perilously close to giving up, but as happens so often in life, just as it seemed that they would never get anywhere or do anything, matters took a sudden turn for the better. And in fact, it was what happened next that turned the Smeezingtons (as they were not yet called) into one of the most sought after songwriting and record producing outfits of their era: for the first time it was suggested to them that they write not for Bruno, but for someone else. Again, like so much in life, it was chance rather than design that brought it about, when a record label heard and, finally, finally, liked one of their songs. But they didn't want Bruno to perform it: they wanted it to go somewhere else. By this time the boys almost didn't care: they were so desperate to make some headway and, crucially, to earn some money, that they would have gone along with just about any suggestion if they thought it would get them anywhere. And anyway, they had no choice. It was a matter of going along with what the record company wanted or handing in the towel.

Just as Philip was to tell the story about being almost too broke to meet Bruno on many occasions, so Bruno had his own party piece when it came to relating how it all took off. "A record label heard a song I'd written for myself, and they wanted to buy it from me for their artist," he said in an interview with *The Guardian.* "I was very, very broke at the time, and as much as I didn't want to sell my song because I wanted to put my own album out, I kind of had no choice: it was either sell the song or move back home to Hawaii. After I sold the song, it kind of opened my eyes – like, man, I don't think these labels want to take a chance on a new artist, they'd rather go with what's working, so it's probably better for me to just start producing for acts they already have." It was in fact actually a breakthrough moment, to say nothing of a very much needed lifeline. The duo got $20,000 for the song, a drop in the ocean of what was to come later – but it was very much needed at the time.

Bruno was coy about what the song was. "Oh, I don't even want to say!" he told *Entertainment Weekly.* "It was a song that they took for a boy band. And then they asked me if I had more songs. I ended up producing a song for Brandy called 'Long Distance'. It just steamrolled into me becoming this producer all of a sudden. Instead of labels calling me up to sign me, they were like, 'Can we have some of our artists come in and work with you guys and write some songs?'" (In actual fact, the song was 'Lost'.)

And now, at last, the industry began to take at least a little bit of notice of the two. Bruno and Philip got their first taste of the big time when they became involved in 'Right Round', a single for the American rapper Flo Rida, inspired by the Dead or Alive hit 'You Spin Me Round (Like A Record)' from 1984, which is indeed sampled in the chorus. But the boys were part of a much bigger setup: other writers included Flo Rida, Dr Luke, Kool Kojak, DJ Frank E, Aaron Bay-Schuck and Dead or Alive themselves, although the very origin of the song came from the Smeezingtons and Bay-Schuck. They put it together with Flo Rida in mind, with Philip later commenting that it was "almost something we had accidentally written in the car one night just hanging out". It led to comparisons with Britney Spears' hit 'If You Seek Amy', also a song involving sex and night clubs.

It was produced by Dr Luke and Kool Kojak, and featured guest vocals from Kesha, who was not credited on the record. "'Right Round' is about a young lady, she might be in the strip club and she's got my head spinning round," Flo Rida told MTV. "Or any young lady that I might see walking past me that's getting my attention. She got it going on! I'm going crazy over her. I might go to the club and make it rain... in the club on her because she got it going on."

The song was to be seen as pretty controversial, not least because of the refrain "You spin my head right round, right round/When you go down, when you go down," a line that Bruno himself said referred to oral sex. Nor did it go down well with the critics. *The New York Times* called it "[b]ionic and empty". Ken Capobianco of *The Boston Globe* said, "His music is pure ear candy that must make Britney envious, yet he wants to come off as a thug." It was "as hard as Jell-O". Alex Fletcher of Digital Spy remarked, "It's pretty difficult to ruin a pop classic, but Flo Rida gives it a pretty good stab here… [it is] filled with more misogyny than a seventies working mens' club… an unpleasant affair that's only saved from the trashcan by its sample. If that were not enough, he added, "The fuzzy synths, electro beats and infectious chorus hook sung by Kesha are almost enough to fool the casual listener into enjoying themselves. But sadly it's never too long before Flo Rida turns up again to spoil things." Simon Vozick-Levinson of *Entertainment Weekly* didn't like it either: it was "a horrendous rap remake of Dead Or Alive's 'You Spin Me Round (Like A Record)'… What does all this say about us as a society? Mainly that we really, really enjoy cheesetastic eighties hair-pop hits in whatever form we can get 'em, I guess."

Not everyone hated it. Fraser McAlpine of the BBC said, "It's one of the fundamental laws of pop, anything which tips a nod to 'You Spin Me Round (Like A Record)' by Dead Or Alive is going to be worth a listen. Even though this is just a song written from the perspective of a randy man watching a pole-dancer and bragging about how much money he has […] in a manner which would make Akon blush, there's just something kind of cute about the whole thing… How can anything too sordid be going on when everyone is bouncing around like they're on spacehoppers?" Bill Lamb of About.com added, "You will hear echoes of another pop classic, but the new song stands on its own feet."

Not that anyone involved would have been too worried about all this negativity: they were too busy crying their way to the bank. The song was a smash success, going to the number one position on the *Billboard* charts in the United States and doing equally well throughout much of the rest of the world. Everyone involved was singing along to the sound of ringing cash tills and although it had been a huge group production, rather than something the two of them had written and produced on their own, it gave the boys their first true taste of success. It also gained them some respect from the rest of the industry. "That was a sample, obviously, but we got our name in there and got some publishing," Bruno told *Entertainment Weekly*. "And it was a number one record. That was our first taste of what could really happen with a hit we hundred-percented."

Behind the scenes, Bay-Schuck continued to push. The duo were as eager as he was to make that final breakthrough, and were receptive to everything he suggested, while at the same time they were continuing to hone their craft. "I just had him writing, writing, writing … it just never stopped," Bay-Schuck told Hitquarters. "Phil and Bruno were willing to write for anything, from Flo Rida to Plies to Trey Songz. He couldn't help but improve as a songwriter and a producer. The more you write, the more you find out what works for you and what works for other artists. We were always exchanging tracks and ideas. It was a monthly process that never stopped and still hasn't even after he was signed. Bruno is always creating."

But it wasn't all work. While he has never been a womaniser per se, Bruno has always liked women and they have always liked him in return. And LA is where to find the pick of the bunch: chock full of would-be models, actresses, whatevers, Bruno was not slow to notice that there were attractive women all over the place. And while he was never going to be tall, Bruno was growing into a spectacularly good-looking man himself, good looks as if designed by a focus group, as one wag put it. Allied to those looks was an easy charm: he might have moved to LA, but Bruno was still a Hawaiian boy at heart, all soft melting glances, living in the moment and going with the flow. He was known to lose his temper in the recording studio, but certainly not when he was out on the town, and for a while, by his own admission, he ran a little wild where women were concerned. He was an exceptionally good-looking up-and-coming pop star. There was no shortage of women to pursue.

But Bruno tired of that particular scene pretty quickly. It was a hollow way to live, even for a young man and, anyway, Bruno had met someone. Her name was Chanel Malvar. Chanel was to be Bruno's first serious relationship: born in Tacoma, WA, she trained as a dancer and gymnast as a child, before turning to dancing professionally in her late teens. She was taken on by a group called Cruz Control before moving to LA in 2003. Chanel and Bruno got together in 2009 and were together for about a year, before breaking up amidst accusations of cheating on both sides, which both in turn denied. Very few details about the relationship have ever been made public, but for a time it was serious and a welcome distraction from the difficulty of making a name for yourself in LA.

But matters were looking up a little for Bruno, and not just romantically. Finally, he had been involved with a hit. While it had shown the boys what could be accomplished with a lot of hard work, it told them something else, too. They wanted to be far more in control than they had been in 'Right Round', where they had been part of a much larger crowd. They didn't just want to write the songs: they wanted to produce them, too. This was becoming a long way from what Bruno had initially started out to do, but increasingly, the future was becoming clear. If he couldn't be a solo artist – not that Bruno had given up on that ambition – he would be part of a production team, churning out hit singles for other performers. And so the setup was almost complete – but not quite. As with the Three Musketeers, there was to be a third person involved, and it was now time for him to come on the scene at last.

Bruno and Philip were very talented songwriters, but if they were going to have the kind of setup they wanted, then they were going to need a record producer on board, too. And in the end, the choice was an easy one. Philip already knew the musician/songwriter/engineer Ari Levine as he had previously worked with him at Levcon Studios, which Levine owned, and so at the turn of 2009, he introduced him to Bruno. It was immediately obvious, just as had been the case with Bruno and Philip, that the two would hit it off. Indeed, the three men seemed to complement one another perfectly: as a trio they gelled instantly although, yet

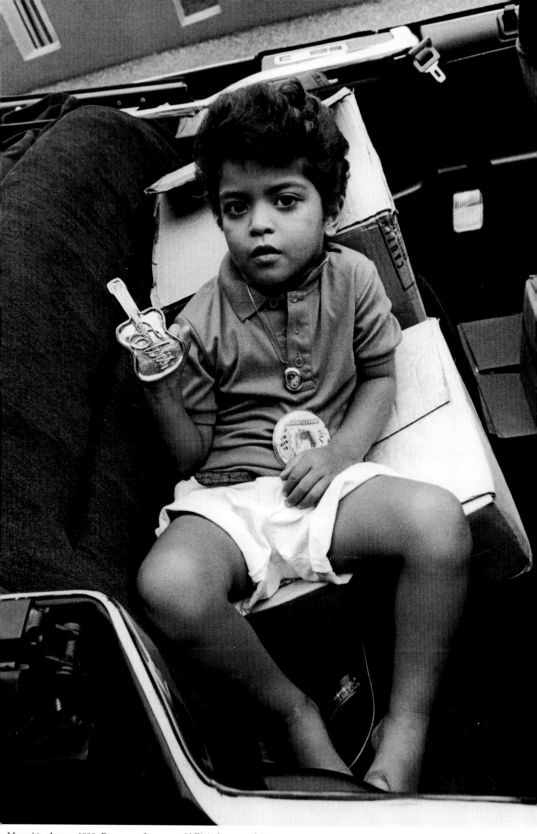

Memphis, August 1990: Bruno as a four-year-old Elvis fan, one of the youngest ever. CATHERINE McGANN/GETTY IMAGES

Young Elvis in Vegas-style jump suit and gold lamé.

The Hernandez clan – back row: mother Bernadette holding baby Presley, dad Peter; front: Tahiti, Bruno, Tiara and Eric.

Bruno's serious afro for the high school prom.

Teenage Bruno with his first band and friends at Roosevelt High School. DENNIS ODA/STAR-BULLETIN

Bruno (left) with his mom and uncle John.

August 2010 and Bruno finds B flat 7th on his Fender guitar.

The Smeezingtons, left to right: Ari Levine, Bruno Mars and Philip Lawrence, at the Grammy Nominations Concert in Los Angeles, December 1, 2010. FRANK TRAPPER/CORBIS

Bruno with R&B star Janelle Monae at the Costume Institute Gala Benefit, celebrating Alexander McQueen at the Metropolitan Museum of Art, New York, May 2, 2011. GREGORY PACE/BEI/REX

Bruno and his band arrive at the 2013 TV Week Logies Awards Ceremony held at the Crown Casino in Melbourne, Australia. KHAP/SPLASH NEWS/CORBIS

Mr Cool: Bruno with his Grammy award for Best Male Pop Vocal Performance for 'Just The Way You Are' at the Staples Center in Los Angeles, February 13, 2011. KEVORK DJANSEZIAN/GETTY IMAGES

Red Hot: Bruno at the Barclays Center in New York, June 29, 2013. BRAD BARKET/GETTY IMAGES FOR ATLANTIC RECORDS

Philip Lawrence, Keri Hilson and Bruno perform at the Grammy celebrations at Bardot in Los Angeles, February 11, 2011.
JOHNNY NUNEZ/WIREIMAGE

Bruno on-stage during the MTV Europe Music Awards 2011 live show at the Odyssey Arena, Belfast, November 6, 2011.

again, they would have to work hard before they finally generated interest from the rest of the music industry. But the combination of talent was now perfect: Ari's instrumental and production talents were exactly what they needed to complement Bruno and Philip's songwriting prowess. The struggle was nearly over, but there was still a way to go. But their personalities meshed perfectly – and they had something else in common, too. Although there is no reason to think this had anything to do with their friendship or personality, all three men are very diminutive in stature. Could that be another factor that strengthened their bond?

Ari, however, was a little different from the other two. Although also versed in music since early childhood, he'd not endured the same desperate struggle as his two new colleagues and was already the co-owner of Levcon Studios, which was to become the trio's base, with his brother and manager, Josh. A year older than Bruno, Ari wasn't a showman like the other two: while Bruno and Philip were only too happy to take centre stage at every possible opportunity, Ari preferred then and now to remain in the background, in the studio. "I don't want to be famous or on stage, I just want to make music," he once said (although in truth, given the company in which he was now moving, he was never going to be able to stay totally anonymous) and that pretty much summed up the man. Like the other two, he had music in his blood: he grew up in Teaneck, New Jersey, playing piano and the drums. At the age of 16, with the permission of his parents, he dropped out of school to do an internship at a New York demo studio. He career flourished from there.

"It was at Mother West Studios, a small facility that records indie bands and so on," he recalled to Soundonsound.com after the boys had become famous. "Not long afterwards, I moved to Los Angeles, where I went to the Los Angeles Recording School, and after that I got an internship in another studio here. I basically worked as a recording engineer, and bought gear from whatever money I could set aside. I then went freelance and took clients with me to different studios, and I'd make friends with a bunch of different people, including studio owners. One studio owner had a small extra room, and I convinced him to let me put my gear in there and work there."

It was a far cry from Bruno and Philip's early experiences: Ari achieved both success and some degree of financial stability right from the start. Indeed, he showed himself to be a pretty good businessman, another talent that would work well with his new colleagues. "After one and a half years, my brother and I had enough equipment to start our own small studio in Hollywood, which is Levcon," he continued. "We started that about six years ago. Initially, I was just making tracks and sending them to songwriters to add top lines to, but once I began working with Bruno and Phil, writing became more organic. We now start all songs we write from scratch, and don't use pre-made tracks or loops any more."

And so, what was to become one of the most successful production teams of the era set to work. But now the next dilemma occurred to them: what, exactly, should they call themselves? If they were going to be presenting themselves as a team, then they needed a name. And so, they came up with one of the most unusual monikers in the business. They would become the Smeezingtons. The way that Bruno told it, it was an obvious name, really: "We don't take ourselves too seriously," he told The Music Mix. "We used to always say in the studio, 'Yo, this is going to be a smash!' And then it turned into, 'This is a smeeze!' Then, 'This is a Smeezington.' We were just like, 'We should just base our whole situation upon this word. How great would it be if record labels were like, 'We have to get the Smeezingtons involved'?"

It was a very clever move. The Smeezingtons was not your average name and it was one to lodge in the memory – preferably a record company's memory. They were beginning to stand out for their musical ability and now their name marked them out as something different too. Marketing, as they were beginning to find out, is everything, and that came down to what they called themselves, too.

Chapter 6

A Star Is Born

By now, they were beginning to make a name for themselves in the industry, although it was very hard work. The three of them were disciplined, ambitious and determined to make it and so 10-hour days in the studio became the norm. They began to work out what would make a hit single, deciding that every song should be like a three-minute movie, with a conflict within it to make it interesting. All were perfectionists: it was not unusual for them to spend months working out exactly what one line should be, so determined were they to get everything exactly right. It was to pay off: although they certainly worked at it, it was not long before the group began to enjoy extraordinary success.

And it helped enormously that there were three of them involved in the process: because they worked well together, they could bounce ideas off one another to find out what really worked. This was still quite new for Bruno and Philip, both of whom might have worked on stage with other people as performers, but on the whole had worked as songwriters alone. The addition of Ari to the mix was making a tremendous difference: with his background and experience they were now coming on faster than ever before. "Ari turned out to be the secret ingredient to what me and Phil were doing," Bruno told the *Huffington Post*. "I'm used to live stuff. So you give me a studio with a bunch of live instruments, I can do it. But radio's not playing that stuff."

Judging one another's reaction, taking on board suggestions and generally pulling together was all working out well, too. If one person was almost there with an idea, but couldn't quite make it work, there was always someone with a suggestion to push it through to fruition – or, of course, to point out that actually, it was never going to work. "There's strength in numbers," Philip accurately told Music Connection. "Especially if they're guys you trust and who know you at your best. I can't always say that the dynamic between us is better [than working alone] but I know that it's different and certainly more effective. If I'm working on an idea by myself, I could be going off in a direction that later I'll discover was wrong. When I'm with the group, they can say, 'Dude, that's kind of corny.'"

The boys were also aware that they really had to engage with their audience, tackle issues that people really did care about. "There are different ways to go about songwriting," Philip continued. "There's the popular radio way and then there's just outright creativity. I don't think one is any better than the other. But even in those two mediums, the one ingredient has to be talking about something that people care about, whether that's love, heartbreak or something political. If you can find a point of view and see it through, that's one thing a song can't be without." It was an attitude that was going to serve them spectacularly well.

Another element in the mix that worked well for the boys was that they also shared the same common influences from their youth. All three loved the Neptunes and Timbaland, the hip-hop makers all three grew up listening to, who are credited with influencing their "throwback" style. Then they had their own individual tastes: Bruno told an increasingly interested industry that his influences had been R&B artists including Keith Sweat, Jodeci, R. Kelly, fifties rock 'n' roll and Motown; as he grew older he also began to enjoy the music of the Police, Led Zeppelin, the Beatles, Billy Joel, Elton John, Michael Jackson, Little Richard and Bob Marley. Philip cited a similar though not identical roster: Elton John, Seal, the Isley Brothers, the Eagles, Led Zeppelin, Stevie Wonder and Billy Joel. They continued to hone their talent, saying that a new song could start with a Levine beat, a Mars guitar melody or a lyrical snippet from Lawrence. And as they started to experience success, they grew in confidence, doing better and better as they went along.

The industry really was sitting up and taking notice now. "Each member of the Smeezingtons – the trio of Bruno Mars, Philip Lawrence and Ari Levine – adds his own special sauce: Lawrence is a melody and lyrics maestro, Levine has recording-engineer smarts, and Mars is, well, Mars, touching everything Smeez-related with his kinetic virtuosity," said *Billboard*. "'Nine times out of 10, Bruno will be on the piano, singing something,' Levine says. 'I'll have a beat going, and Philip will be figuring out lyrics and melody. Whatever sparks something, we just try not to mess it up.'" Not much chance of that.

All three tried to explain the dynamic, for whatever was going on in that studio, it clearly worked. "We're melody guys, we sing," Philip told MTV. "That's kind of our main focus, to have really good, memorable melodies. We'll go into the studio, and [Mars will] start playing the piano and I'll start freestyling or vice versa. We're heavily influenced by the eighties [sound]."

To begin with, the boys focused mainly on R&B, working with acts including Mike Posner, Cobra Starship, Chad Hugo and Lupe Fiasco. So far, so not very interesting – these collaborations didn't make much of an impact. But their work became increasingly high profile when further artists they collaborated with included Flo Rida (again), Lil Wayne, Wiz Khalifa and CeeLo Green. And then came the Sugababes, and a giant leap forward in their fortunes once more.

The Sugababes, an English girl group, were working on their seventh album, entitled, for obvious reasons, *Sweet 7*. They wanted a lead single with a bright, upbeat electropop feel, and so employed Bruno, Philip, Ari, Fred Fairbrass, Richard Fairbrass and Rob Manzoli to write it, although to be more accurate, those latter three, the members of Right Said Fred, had already written 'I'm Too Sexy', which featured on the new song. The Smeezingtons alone produced it: it was to be the making of them.

According to band member Keisha Buchanan, the single almost came about by accident. "The producers were messing around going, 'I'm too sexy for the studio'," she said in an interview with Teletext. "We were like, 'That sounds cool', and [the producer] said, 'You remember that Right Said Fred song?' We were like, 'Do you think we can do it?' By accident it came together." It certainly did.

'Get Sexy' came out on August 30, 2009, and as with Bruno and Philip's earlier outing with Flo Rida, received mixed reviews and rapturous sales. Caroline Sullivan of *The Guardian* said it was a "grinding, fiercely catchy R&B number". David Balls of Digital Spy opined, "'Get Sexy' is a dancefloor stomper that nestles somewhere between 'Boom Boom Pow' and 'Bonkers' in its blend of electropop, techno and R&B sounds. It may not be massively original, nor an instant classic to rival 'About You Now' or 'Push The Button', but with a Right Said Fred-sampling hook, a thundering chorus and plenty of attitude – most noticeably from Amelle – it returns Sugababes right to the forefront of the pop landscape."

Popjustice said: "'Get Sexy' is a punchy, explosive pop single which, while not being quite as adventurous as it thinks it is, could never be described as pedestrian." Fraser McAlpine of the BBC didn't like it: it was "a mess" which has "not bothered to make it rhyme" in the way the original, 'I'm Too Sexy' did. "The 'shut up and watch me walk' bit is pilfered from the Ting Tings. [...] [Amelle's 'silly boys' bit – which is brilliant, by the way – may have more than a passing acquaintance with 'My Humps'. [...] the chorus is desperate for someone to scream 'will.i.am drop the beat now'."

As before, everyone wept all the way to the bank, with the song selling massively well and pushing the Smeezingtons' star ever higher into the ascendant. It was, however, notable in that it marked the end of Keisha Buchanan's involvement with the Sugababes: she left the group soon after. For the Smeezingtons, however, it was an unmitigated triumph. Given that the song did well all over the world, it introduced them to an international audience, flung open doors that until then had been closed and had record labels taking an interest of the sort they'd never shown before. It had been a hard slog, but it was now all coming together beautifully, and the Smeezingtons were going to become one of the most sought-after outfits in the business, rolling out one hit after another for the likes of Alexandra Burke, Travie McCoy, Adam Levine, Brandy and Sean Kingston. And Bruno, one of its founding members, was going to become an international star.

Indeed, it was around this time that Bruno finally began to appear on some of the recordings he was involved with, although initially on a small scale. His first musical appearance was on Far East Movement's second studio album, *Animal*, on the track '3D', and he was also to be found on pastor and hip-hop artist Jaeson Ma's debut single, 'Love'. Meanwhile, work with the Smeezingstons, who were increasingly being spoken of as movers and shakers in the business, went on: the trio worked on numbers that massively increased their profile because they were associated with some very high-profile sporting events. 'Wavin' Flag' by the Somali-Canadian artist K'Naan was one of theirs and was chosen for the theme song for the 2010 FIFA World Cup, while Matisyahu's 'One Day' was chosen as NBC's 2010 Winter Olympics theme song. The boys were starting to be in the right place at the right time and other people were noticing it too.

"K'Naan had the song 'Wavin' Flag' for a while," Bruno told *Entertainment Weekly* in a 2010 interview. "He was performing that hook, 'When I get older, I will be stronger...' And he never got into the studio and produced it. He called us and asked if we wanted to take a crack at it. It turned out beautifully and made his album. K'Naan called us later and said, 'Hey, I have this opportunity. Coca Cola is really interested in getting 'Flag'. I want to get back in the studio with you guys and revamp it.' We got the word that they love it. They're going for it. The version that they'll play is real tribal with African drums. It's a whole stadium kind of thing. Matisyahu's song 'One Day' was NBC's 2010 Winter Olympic theme song. That's another song we wrote and produced. It's kind of been the best year of our lives."

That was understating it: it was to be a year that changed all their lives. Following Bruno's successes, he had finally been signed to Atlantic Records and the time was coming for him to make his debut. The vehicle was to be 'Nothin' On You', the debut singer by the rapper B.o.B., aka Bobby Ray Simmons from North Carolina, who had been discovered in 2006, but who was only now about to make his debut. The Smeezingtons had got involved: Aaron Bay-Schuck had encouraged them to develop one of the tunes he'd heard them humming and in its earliest version the song consisted of a chorus-only number that had Bruno singing against a guitar track. (This was also how the Travie McCoy number 'Billionaire' had its gestation.) Shortly afterwards B.o.B. joined them in the studio to complete the full song.

Bruno and Philip gave an interview to MTV, explaining exactly how it all came about. "Me and Phil always had that hook," said Bruno, humming to illustrate the point.

"It was a different melody at first, though," Lawrence added.

"So one day our other partner – the Silent Bob of the Smeezingtons – Ari, he walked into the studio and said he programmed the drums [over]," Bruno continued. "It had this old-school hip-hop beat. I said, 'Gimme the piano,' and that was the first thing I started playing. Magically, that melody worked with this track we were doing."

So, this was to be another Smeezingtons production number, but this time there was going to be a little difference. Bruno himself was going to sing on the track, finally proving, to the music industry once and for all that here was a seriously talented artist who was capable of making the grade himself. When the record came out, several people in the industry suggested that there was some vanity performing involved, that one of the producers also fancied a moment in the limelight, but in actual fact, of course, that was far from the truth. The plan, right from the start, had been for Bruno to make it as a solo performer and everyone involved had simply been waiting for the right time and the right vehicle. And, at long last, this was it.

But it nearly didn't happen. Years later, Bruno told *Entertainment Weekly* that a music industry boss, who has never been named, originally thought that Bruno was the wrong colour. "He goes, 'Oh man, oh man, what a song,'" Bruno said. "You know what kind of white artist we could break with this? Blond hair, blue eyes, we could make this kid the next thing! It was just kinda sad. It was like, 'Man, what about the kid that played you the song and wrote it and produced it... what about that guy?'" Further, it made him feel like "a mutant. Even with that song in my back pocket to seal the deal, things like that are coming out of people's mouths. It made me feel like I wasn't even in the room."

In the event, the song was an absolute smash, soaring to number one in the UK, the United States and the Netherlands and being nominated for three Grammys, including Record of the Year for the 53rd Grammy awards. The public loved it. "The way Megan Fox oozes trampish sex appeal, or your boyfriend oozes garlic the morning after a good old Ruby [Ruby Murry is cockney rhyming slang for curry], some songs just ooze 'smash'," is what Digital Spy had to say about it. "A fine example is 'Nothin' On You', the debut single from Atlanta-based rapper B.o.B. and already a platinum-plated chart-topper across the pond. In fact, with its fat 'n' satisfying beats, dreamy piano line and brilliant hook, courtesy of fellow newcomer Bruno Mars, it could be rap's biggest crowd-pleaser since Jay teamed up with Alicia." Note the fact that Bruno got a mention: right from the start it was evident that he was going to benefit from the song's success just as much as B.o.B.

But history could have been so different, for originally the song wasn't meant for B.o.B at all. It had actually been intended for Lupe Fiasco. The Chicago-born rapper, real name Wasalu Muhammad Jaco, had been planning on releasing the record as a single, and it was only a creative disagreement with his record label that made Atlantic drop plans to use him and give the song to one of its other artists instead.

"I was actually working on a session in Chung King [Studios], and [Atlantic Records chairman] Craig Kallman called me during that session with that particular track, to work on it for Lupe Fiasco," the producer Jim Jonsin told MTV. "I told Craig, 'I like the song a lot. It's a smash and could be somebody's single. But it's not Lupe's record. I need this record for B.o.B. Please give this record to B.o.B.' I guess they went through whoever they went through, convinced whoever they needed to, and it got to B.o.B."

And what a wise decision that turned out to be. The combination of B.o.B. and Bruno was a potent one, forming the basis of not one but two stellar careers and in danger of confusing the public as to which one was the real star. For Bruno, too, it was a moment to savour: after all these years working for other people and getting nowhere on his own account, he was finally being vindicated, finally showing all the people who said he'd never make it as a solo act that they were wrong. Jubilant is not too strong a word to describe his state of mind, and if anyone had earned this success, then it was Bruno. And what a success it was turning out to be.

But the scale of it all took everyone by surprise – no one had realised what a hit they had on their hands. "We really didn't expect it to have the dramatic impact it had, nor how fast it happened," B.o.B told MTV. "Me and my managers, B. Rich and TJ, we still look at each other speechless. We always aim to be successful. But when the by-product exceeds your expectations – when usually you barely make the basket with what you want – the gratitude is through the roof. It's literally a dream come true."

Bruno was by now in another experience that was new to him. On the one hand he had people in the music industry thinking that he was a producer who would like a share of the limelight, whereas now, on the other, he had members of the public who thought he was a performer and who had no idea that he had been responsible for writing and producing the record, too. When this information leaked out, interest in him only began to grow. In an era of reality stars, people pitched into the limelight with little experience and no way of coping with their new-found fame, to say nothing of negligible talent and very little chance of staying the course, Bruno was the real thing. He was a singer-songwriter who had paid his dues and come up the hard way and now he was getting his reward.

It certainly didn't hurt that Bruno looked every inch the pop star. Olive skin, high cheekbones, shiny white teeth – Bruno was certainly suitable as teen idol material, more than capable of holding his own with other posters on many a teenage girl's wall. But he had an equally big fanbase among men – and older audiences, come to that. Ironically, given that the music industry had not known quite how to classify him when he first appeared in their midst, now this was turned to his advantage, given that he had such widespread appeal. That very eclectic musical background was another bonus too, for just as younger fans related to the music Bruno was now himself creating, so older ones shared the same tastes he'd had when he was growing up.

But what really set him apart was that he was as much of a songwriter as he was a singer, and like so many writers was learning to channel his own personal experiences into his work. Bruno admitted that the song had been born from his amorous adventures, which he was still being extremely coy about. "Every song I write has to do with a real-life experience, whether it's at the time or me back-tracking to how I felt at another moment," he told MidWeek. "So, yeah, it was about someone - let's leave it at that. It was not to be the last song he wrote with a particular woman in mind either. As Bruno's love life developed, so did the extent to which it would influence his art.

It wasn't just Bruno who was pleased: the team he had been working with was pretty thrilled, too. In the face of some indifference from the music industry they'd stuck up for their man and it wasn't just Bruno who was vindicated – they were too. And they had been working behind the scenes just as hard as Bruno to achieve the results that they finally got. A great deal of planning had gone into it, and although no one could have prophesied with certainty quite how well it would turn out, neither was it all totally down to chance.

The only person who was not ecstatic was Lupe Fiasco, who went very public about his anger that the song had been taken away from him. "That was the tipping point," he said in an interview with *The Guardian*, in which he revealed that Atlantic chairman Craig Kallman had told him his verses and performance were "wack". "It was less about the bruised ego but more the audacity of it. It was mentally destructive. I say it with a certain laissez-faire now because I'm past it, but back then, hearin' that shit, it fucked me up. I was super-depressed, lightly suicidal, at moments medium suicidal – and if not suicidal, willing to just walk away from it all completely." It had clearly been a painful episode for him and his own version of the song eventually leaked out to the public, too.

With that episode firmly in the bag, Bruno needed a follow-up quickly to consolidate his success, and he got it in the form of another collaboration, this time with Travie McCoy. The rapper and lead singer of the rap rock band Gym Class Heroes was releasing his solo album *Lazarus* in 2010, and was about to release the lead single from it: it was to be 'Billionaire', once again featuring Bruno. Again it came from the Smeezingtons' stable, which again served to boost Bruno's reputation as both a singer and a songwriter and again the song, in which the singer imagines what it would be like to be a billionaire, was born of his personal experience.

"Me and Ari Levine went out to London to work on producing and writing for an artist," Bruno told *Billboard*. "We had per diems, so they gave us £250 [a few hundred dollars] each to live off of for 11 days. And everything there was so expensive. We were like, 'Is this the biggest mistake we've ever made? We thought we were broke in California; what are we going to do here?' So we've got no money, and I'm walking the streets and came up with, 'I wanna be a billionaire, so frickin' bad.'"

However, some sensitivity was needed here. The financial downturn had started two years earlier and a lot of people all over the world were still suffering and no one involved wanted to appear crass. They were determined to avoid superficial lyrics: "There's something to sing about here; if I was in the position to have a ridiculous amount of money, would I be selfish or selfless?' I just took that concept and ran with it," Travie told *The Oakland Press*.

The song had been created in the course of a week-long studio session in the summer of 2009, the same session that had produced 'Nothin' On You'. Travie later joined the Smeezingtons in the studio to put the finishing touches on it all. There was the original version of the song and a radio one, which replaced the world "fucking" with "freaking" and an official remix featuring Bruno, his Nappy Boy labelmates T-Pain and R&B group One Chance and Atlanta-based rapper Gucci Mane, alongside various other remixes, including a Hawaiian one by a band called Big Every Time.

The accompanying video was very much on the theme of helping others out. It opened with Bruno playing a guitar while sitting on a wall in Venice Beach before moving on to a shot in which Travie is driving a Mini Cooper with Bruno in the passenger seat. Travie goes on to help four people: he starts by giving one guy a skateboard, then buys an unknown artist's CD, moves on to getting out of the car and giving the keys to a teenager trying to hitchhike to New York and finally replenishing the spray-paint supply of a graffiti artist. As the video draws to a close, a party is pictured that has run out of beer; Bruno and Travie turn up with new supplies and the party kicks off again.

It was another worldwide hit and by now Bruno's mellifluous tones and film-star good looks were beginning to attract a good deal of attention beyond the music industry. And it was also noted in some quarters that Bruno's presence on a track meant that it was increasingly certain to become a hit. "Travie McCoy is taking a cue from B.o.B, enlisting singer Bruno Mars (featured on B.o.B's 'Nothin' On You') for his solo debut single, 'Billionaire'," wrote Melanie Bertoldi in *Billboard*. "Formerly known as Travis, the Gym Class Heroes frontman fantasises about success over a nimble, reggae-tinged rhythm. He imagines helping New Orleans after Hurricane Katrina and becoming the male version of Oprah Winfrey, and if you 'give Travie a wish list,' he raps, he'd 'probably pull an Angelina and Brad Pitt/ And adopt a bunch of babies that ain't never had shit.' The goals that Mars sings of are a little more self-interested. 'I see my name in shining lights,' he croons, expressing his desire to be a *Forbes* magazine cover boy in the same breath. The message may be inconsistent, but the beat still goes down smoothly." It was an accurate prediction, too, on Bruno's part, as to what lay ahead.

Nick Levine on Digital Spy liked it too, although he was a little less complimentary about Bruno's contribution. "'I wanna be a billionaire so fucking bad,' croons Bruno Mars on the one-listen hook that kicks off 'Billionaire', but before you think, 'Oh shit, not *another* witless hip-hop paean to materialism', just listen to the rhymes from the man whose debut solo single this *actually* is," he wrote. "For Gym Class Heroes frontman / survivor of The Katy Perry Experience Travie McCoy wants to be filthy rich not just so he can play basketball with the President, but also so he can do a whole loada good deeds. 'I'd probably pull an Angelina and Brad Pitt / And adopt a bunch of babies that ain't never had shit,' he raps over a brassy reggae-pop groove that recalls No Doubt's 2002 hit 'Underneath It All'. The result? A summer pop treat so sweet and tasty it's even possible to forgive McCoy's slightly irritating change of billing – just as long as he doesn't start styling himself Trav-E Trav any time soon."

It might have been Travie's debut single, but it was the Smeezingtons who wrote and produced it and the photogenic Bruno, in particular, was by now getting so much attention that it was clear his time was nearly here. Of course, he had been very much a secondary presence on them, but he himself realised that was right, in one interview saying, "I think those songs weren't meant to be full-sung songs. If I'd sung all on 'Nothin' On You' it might've sounded like some nineties R&B." Whatever the truth of that, he was sensible enough to know that he'd been offered a chance and now, at long last, was receiving the attention he deserved.

By now, of course, it was just a matter of time before Bruno released his first single, and that came about on May 11, 2010. He recorded a debut EP entitled *It's Better If You Don't Understand*, a title taken from the last line of the single it produced, 'The Other Side', with the three other tracks being 'Somewhere In Brooklyn' (many critics' favourite track), 'Count On Me' and 'Talking To The Moon'. 'The Other Side' also featured guest vocals, in this case from Bruno's old friend B.o.B. as well as CeeLo Green. Everything on it was eventually included in his debut album, of which more anon and while its success was modest, with the EP peaking at number 99 on the *Billboard* 200 and 97 on the UK singles chart, it was enough to show that Bruno was on his way.

The industry was beginning to realise this too. The accompanying video was a comment on what was happening to Bruno: "The video takes us through what is now a typical day in Mars' life, from posing at a high-production value photo shoot to strumming on an empty sidewalk," said *Billboard*. "Mars, who teams up with CeeLo and B.o.B. for the track, exhibits his multi-instrumentalist talents throughout: he lightly feels the keys of a stand-up piano, hops in front of a retro microphone with his guitar and taps the snare of a bright blue drum set, which is sometimes played by a cute little boy in striped overalls." It was not only a description of the video – it was an acceptance that a new star had been born.

Other people clearly thought so too. "It's that voice that grabs your attention in the beginning," wrote Bill Lamb on about. com. "The sweet sound with a bit of a street edge in Bruno Mars' singing is at the heart of B.o.B.'s massive number one hit 'Nothin' On You' as well as Travie McCoy's smash in progress 'Billionaire'. Now a four song EP has been pushed out quickly to capitalise on interest in this upcoming serious talent. Fortunately, these songs more than uphold the promise he has shown on the guest appearances. Almost any serious pop fan will find a lot to like here."

David Jeffries on allmusic.com felt the same. "By the time of his official debut release, Bruno Mars was already known as a genre-defying (hip-hop/pop/R&B) triple-threat (singer/ songwriter/producer) of a hitmaker (co-writer of Flo Rida's 'Right Round'/co-writer and guest vocalist on B.o.B.'s 'Nothin' On You')," he wrote. "Instead of introducing his solo career with the guest-star filled, everywhere-at-once, and possibly-too-big album, someone made the brilliant decision to slowly introduce him with this humble EP, a four-song and surprisingly sparse effort that leans towards pop while focusing on the man's songwriting."

It goes without saying that this was a Smeezingtons production, although plenty of other industry talent had been brought in as well. Now that Bruno finally had his own record out, nothing was being left to chance. But this was it: this is what Bruno had been working for and waiting for – he was finally a recording artist in his own right. It was all a far cry from those days as an infant Elvis impersonator, or indeed the early days in LA, so broke he had to sell his instruments and nearly decided to go home. Bruno was now at last to be introduced to the upside of success: the fame, the wealth and the privilege that fall into the laps of those who have made their mark. But fame and success have a downside too, as Bruno was soon to discover in that Las Vegas court room.

Chapter 7

Fringe Benefits

Bruno was a gifted songwriter: of that there was clearly no doubt. As he continued to create music for some of the biggest names of the day, he was building up his contacts, forging ahead with some important relationships and learning his way about town. But, of course, he was working in show business. And show business is full of beautiful women. Bruno, who had had an eye for the ladies ever since he climbed out of the pram, had noticed this. And while he has always been discrete about his liaisons, information about some of his romantic life did seep out.

One of the most significant of these took place around 2009, just before he hit the big time. Rita Ora was a British singer-songwriter and actress, originally of Kosovar-Albanian stock, who was to go on to have success of a type that would rival Bruno's, going on to become the artist with the most number one singles in the UK in 2013. But that was in the future. Back in 2009, she was just another struggling singer, albeit one for whom the music industry foresaw a great future. And so they brought one of the hottest songwriters in town to write some material for her. His name was Bruno Mars.

The wider world didn't know about it at the time, but then, why would they? Both Bruno and Rita were totally unknown, and no one would have been interested anyway. But for the two of them, it was, albeit briefly, a big deal. "It was love at first sight, such a great experience," Rita told *The Sun*, in an interview in 2012 that provoked some astonishment, given that no one had guessed at the story she had to tell. "We met in 2009. I was 18 and starting out at Roc Nation. Bruno was unknown back then too. He was a struggling songwriter hired to write songs for me. I thought, 'Wow, that's just the world's greatest guy!'"

The feeling was mutual. Bruno was just coming out of what had been a very low point in his life, and as the years of rejection melted into the distance, with the growing acclaim he was receiving from his peers, life was looking up. And that applied to his personal life, too. The relationship prospered, albeit briefly, with Rita later revealing that Bruno had in fact been her first love. Bruno, of course, had had girlfriends before Rita, but he was serious about her, too.

But it was not to last. There was just too much going on in both their lives: you need time to build up a relationship and both were so busy pushing themselves and their careers, that they eventually parted. "Our time together was wonderful. But once we got famous, work got in the way. We ended it last year," Rita continued. "But we remained close. And when we were together we were so happy." Indeed, the two of them continued to bump into one another at industry events: it was all extremely amicable.

Indeed, a star had been born. As so often in these cases, to the outside world it looked as if Bruno was an overnight sensation, an artist who appeared out of nowhere to massive critical acclaim, but the reality was that everyone involved had spent years planning for this to happen. Bruno himself had paid his dues time and time again: this time round there was to be no repeat of the Motown fiasco, in which he had simply been too young and inexperienced to make a go of the contract. He'd been honing his skills for years, turning into not only a fine singer but an extremely talented songwriter. Bruno was something of a perfectionist, insisting that the Smeezingtons spent months, sometimes literally, in the studio in order to get something completely right, but that perfectionism was clearly paying off.

Bruno was not quite done with collaborations, however. Next up was another collaboration with CeeLo Green, entitled variously 'Fuck You', 'Forget You' or 'FU', depending on whether it was being broadcast. The first of these was replete with profanities aplenty, the second got rid of the worst, these being "fuck", "shit", "ass" and "nigga" while 'FU' was a far more sanitised version of the song. There were to be two further versions, 'Fuck You (Heartbreak)' featuring the rapper 50 Cent, of which CeeLo performed a remix on *The Colbert Report*, and 'Thank You', in which the song was rewritten as a tribute to firefighters. This had new lyrics, which mentioned the fact that CeeLo's own mother had been a firefighter.

Although CeeLo was to reveal that the song was aimed at the music industry itself, the accompanying video featured a far more conventional setup, in that it was based around romantic rejection.

The extremely lively video was shot in a fifties-style diner, centring on a girl CeeLo fancies called the Heartbreaker, and with a chorus of girls wearing green dresses somewhat reminiscent of the Supremes. It starts with a young CeeLo going into the diner with his parents and approaching the Heartbreaker, who is with another boy. He offers to let the Heartbreaker play with his toy garbage truck, but she ignores him and walks away with the other boy, who has a toy Ferrari F40. It then fast forwards a few years: by now CeeLo is at high school, working in the diner as a chef. He tries to woo the Heartbreaker with a bouquet of flowers but slips on a plate of French fries that had been deliberately dropped by another boy. The flowers fly out of his hand and land on a much younger girl's lap.

We then fast forward a few years more, where CeeLo is at college. He is studying in the diner with another woman, possibly his music tutor, before trying to woo the Heartbreaker by having the waitress draw a heart-shaped ketchup mark on her hot dog plate. However, the Heartbreaker approaches him with a basket of fries and spills them, leaving a large ketchup stain on his shirt.

We then jump to the present day, where CeeLo has grown up and is now the Lady Killer, something emphasised by the fact that he has a smart Cadillac Eldorado. He drives past the diner to find the Heartbreaker working there, sweeping the front entrance while others are dancing behind her. CeeLo waves at the Heartbreaker before driving away. Everyone got their just deserts: the Heartbreaker is reduced to the status of domestic drudge, while CeeLo is revelling in fame, riches and female attention. It's not hard to see how it could stand for the music industry as a whole and it gained considerable kudos for delivering what was, after all, a very withering put-down in one of the most upbeat tunes of the year.

The song was a global hit, which did no harm to Bruno's growing reputation. The critics liked it, too. "It's as sunny as a sixties Motown hit and as expletive-laden as an early Eminem song, a combination that fits the singer's sky-high vocals and offbeat sense of humour well," wrote Jason Lipshutz in *Billboard*. "Over a twinkling piano line, bumping bass and steady percussion, Green shakes off a failed relationship with a gold digger by packing the simple pleasures of old-school soul music into tongue-in-cheek verses and a suitably soaring chorus."

Over on Digital Spy, Nick Levine awarded it four out of five stars, writing: "As its title suggests, 'Fuck You' is essentially a middle finger extending from the fist of a pop single — and a gloriously catchy Motown stomper of a pop single at that."

And Alexandra Patsavas, music supervisor for the *Twilight* films, was full of praise for Bruno, complementing him on his ability to veer between "a beautifully crafted pop song exquisitely sung" and the likes of CeeLo's 'Fuck You'. "How sublime that an artist can travel so fluidly between humour and earnestness," she continued, but of course, Bruno had had quite a lot of practice in writing many songs in many different styles and genres by now. The tune was admittedly catchy and went on to win a Grammy, while being named the number one song of 2010 by *Time*. Bruno was thrilled, although he was becoming considerably more accustomed to success now than he had been previously.

He was now in demand pretty much everywhere. Appearing at 2010's MTV Video Music Awards, it was Bruno who came on stage first to kick off 'Nothin' On You' before crying, "Give it up to my homie B.o.B.!" The crowd roared its enthusiasm, but the enthusiasm was as much for Bruno as B.o.B. He was visibly growing in stature, increasingly confident and assured in front of an audience (although, of course, most of his new admirers didn't know he'd been performing in front of audiences all of his life) and beginning to accept that his dreams were finally coming true.

And now it was time for the big one: Bruno's first album. This had always been in the pipeline, but given his recent, massive success, everyone involved was keen to get it out while the other hits he had worked on were still in the charts. There was nothing like striking while the iron was hot and you couldn't get much hotter than Bruno at this point, so there was no time to be lost. And so his debut album, *Doo-Wops & Hooligans*, came out in October 2010, just a few months after the lead single from it, 'Just The Way You Are', appeared in July of that year.

'Just The Way You Are' was a stellar success, confirming Bruno as the standout talent to emerge that year. It went to number one in the States, performed well globally, won a Grammy for the Best Male Pop Vocal Performance in 2011 and propelled him from the talented ranks of the music industry to first-rank stardom. It was written by the Smeezingtons, Khalil Walton and Needlz and Bruno himself told 4Music.com, "I'm a big fan of simple songs. When we wrote 'Just The Way You Are', I wasn't thinking of anything deep or poetic. I was telling a story. Get ready to fall in love!"

By this time there really was a huge amount of interest in Bruno and he was now being called on to give frequent interviews about his inspiration and how he came up with the ideas. Bruno was happy to oblige. Having been ignored by the industry so long, he was only too pleased to talk about how he did his work, and so he gave another interview to bluesandsoul.com, talking about how the song had come about.

"Well, I'm a big fan of songs like Joe Cocker's 'You Are So Beautiful' and Eric Clapton's 'Wonderful Tonight' – songs that go straight to the point," he said. "You know, there's no mind-boggling lyrics or twists in the story – they just come directly from the heart. And to me 'Just The Way You Are' is one of those songs! There's nothing mind-blowing about it. I'm just telling a woman she looks beautiful the way she is – and, let's be honest, what woman doesn't wanna hear those lyrics?!... I mean, that's why I've been singing those kinda songs to get girls since I was nine years old!"

There spoke Bruno the ladies' man. But he was right: the theme was universal and it spoke to men and women alike. Indeed, according to the man himself, it could even be used as a kind of relationship counsellor. "And because of what it says, it's also a song that can help guys stop getting into fights with their girl!" he continued. "Like you'll be getting ready to go out to a movie and the girl will be in the bathroom doing their hair, putting on 10 different outfits... And the guy's like 'Babe, come on! Let's go! You look fine with what you've got on!'... And it can all escalate into one big old fight! So in that situation 'Just The Way You Are' is the ideal song for guys to dedicate to their girl! If they don't know exactly what to say they can just play the record!" Pragmatic – but true.

Of course, an awful lot of other people had been involved. Many more careers than Bruno's were riding on this – there was a whole group of people who had been championing him for years and now they were all to be vindicated, too. Bruno was exceedingly talented, there was no doubt about that, but he had also been very lucky to get some other serious players in the music business on board. And the industry was very curious to know what their take on it was, too.

"We had about half of the album done when 'Just The Way You Are' was created but as soon as Bruno finished it we knew we had the first single," Aaron Bay-Schuck told Hitquarters. com. "I had never felt the way I did when I first heard that song. I just knew. It was so special. It had everything we could want in a first single for Bruno. The track had a bit of a left of centre, hip, cool, organic hip-hop drum break, a vibe that Bruno loved and had touched on with 'Nothin' On You'. It didn't sound like anything else on the radio. It was a song written for females but one that every guy who ever had a girlfriend could relate to. It had a massive chorus, an instantly memorable melody and lyric – it just really stuck out compared to all the records on the album and was a natural transition from the B.o.B and Travie McCoy songs."

Ari Levine, while continuing to prefer to be in the background, also gave his take on how the song came about. "Needlz had a track with a melody idea by Khalil Walton that was presented to us by one of the A&R guys," he told soundonsound.com. "Bruno and Phil came up with the chorus, and then Needlz sent us the files and we replaced a bunch of sounds with our sounds and I programmed drums in the MPC, and we wrote the rest of the song. I never met Needlz or Walton."

Rather ironically, poor old Lupe Fiasco featured in this story, too. Needlz had been working with Lupe, looking for a song for him, and Bruno was drafted in to work on it. The result was 'Just The Way You Are' and Lupe was all set to go forward with it – until Bruno decided to keep it for himself. This time Lupe did not go public with a complaint – after Bruno's success it would have been churlish to do so – but it was hard to escape the conclusion that he would have been pleased, at the very least, if the plan had not been changed.

The song was recorded at the Larrabee Sound Studios in Hollywood, with Ari and Bruno playing all the instruments on the track and recording them before the song and seven remixes were released. A ballad in style, it received high critical acclaim: Megan Vick from *Billboard* loved it. "Over a breezy piano and vaguely hip-hop breakbeat, Mars professes his love for a beautiful girl who occupies his dreams," she wrote. "Mars pens lyrics that aim to make female listeners feel nothing short of perfect in their own skin. With its steady, danceable pulse and singalong chorus, Mars has created a feel-good jam that should establish him as a solo contender in his own right."

Leah Greenblatt of *Entertainment Weekly* said that the song was a "sweetly smitten ballad", while Nick Levin from Digital Spy felt that it was an "instant classic feel to 'Empire State Of Mind'". *The Guardian*'s Paul Lester said it was about "a girl Mars could kiss all day". Tim Sendra of allmusic called the debut single "lushly romantic". Scott Kara in the *New Zealand Herald* said the song was a "ballad boogie".

There was the odd dissenting voice: Nima Baniamer from Contactmusic.com wrote that "there is nothing about the single that makes Bruno Mars stand out from all the other R&B artists dominating the charts at the moment", adding, "The song never builds to any climax and it simply falls a bit flat, coming across quite corny and cheesy."

The accompanying video was directed by Ethan Lander – who said of Bruno, "That charisma that he has, you can't teach" – and featured the Peruvian-born actress Nathalie Kelley. It starts with Kelley listening to 'Just the Way You Are' on her Walkman as Bruno walks in; he promptly stops the tape player and begins singing himself. As the instrumental portion of the song begins, Bruno pulls the tape out of the cassette and arranges it into letters forming his name followed by the song title. He then forms a picture of a drum, again on the table, using the tape. Additional images along the same kind of theme crop up throughout the video including a portrait of Mars as well as one of Kelley blinking her eyes and smiling as he continues singing. Most of the images are animated, including a bell which Mars rings with his fingers in synchronisation with the chimes near the end of the song. Finally, he finishes the song while singing and playing an upright piano while Kelley watches and smiles. The video was inspired by the artwork of Erika Iris Simmons. It was as popular as the song: "Producer/songwriter and now breakout solo star Bruno Mars released the video for his mid-tempo love song 'Just The Way You Are' this morning," *Billboard* announced. "It's been decades since cassette tapes have been used for music. So Mars finds a suave way to use the retro tech in the clip, yanking out the tape to draw pictures of his love interest. The video is just as sweet as the track itself."

That Grammy and a number of other awards soon followed. As if to underline the full scale of his achievement, in both 2011 and 2012 it won Most Performed Song and in the latter year, Song of the Year, ultimately selling over 12.5 million copies, making it one of the best-selling singles of all time. *Billboard* ranked it number 74 in a list of the 100 biggest Hot 100 hits ever.

But again, all of this was no accident. A huge amount of time and thought had been devoted to how best to launch Bruno: it had been planned with the precision of a military manoeuvre. In these days of instant stardom, they really had only one chance, and they had to get it right. It was also important to take into account all the various platforms on which it would appear. "It was also a multi-format song. What makes him so special is that he can live on a lot of different radio formats," Aaron Bay-Schuck told Hitquarters.com. "You don't want to let radio dictate who you want to be as an artist but it's a very important thing to consider. Bruno is an act that was breaking on pop radio and it's very hard to be considered a genuine and real artist when people are first hearing your song on Top 40 radio when they don't know anything about you. Sometimes it is good to be on the other radio formats before, because they have a bit more loyalty to the artists they are breaking and really secure a fanbase before crossing over to pop radio. Bruno is a special artist because he is such an incredible live performer so it's been a blessing to have these big pop records, but at the same time he's touring organically underneath all of them to really build that fanbase and really being considered and seen as a legitimate artist – that he's not just a guy that is featured on a couple of big songs. There's some real depth to him."

For Bruno, of course, something else was at stake. He had craved fame for years and was finally realising his great ambition, but at the same time he was also having to learn to be in the public eye. No matter how much anyone wants it, no one can understand what the actual reality of fame is like until it hits them, and it is only then that they need to learn how to cope. Bruno had now entered the world where he had to be cautious about what he did or said in public, and about the people with whom he surrounded himself. In the era of the camera phone, little could be kept entirely secret; on top of that there were those, such as the people caught up in the Vegas incident, who were going to want to do him down. But in those first heady days, when Bruno's face was beginning to appear all over the media and online, he could barely hide his delight at the way everything had turned out.

"It's been incredible so far – you never have any idea how a song's going to do," he told Digital Spy. "That song's been up against Eminem, Rihanna and some other real heavyweights. It's very hard to get a number one record and it's all about timing, the stars and a lot of behind-the-scenes talent! I try and stay away from all the label politics. I just write songs and see what they do with them." It was a modest assessment of a career that had just turned stellar and the tables were beginning to turn. It wasn't so much a case of Bruno keeping the record bosses sweet as the label making sure its new star continued to be a happy man.

It was around this time that Bruno was arrested in Las Vegas, however; a wake-up call if ever there was one about the dangers of beginning to believe your own publicity. Despite the unpleasantness of the whole affair, and the lingering suspicion that he had been set up, Bruno, as has been related earlier, coped and began to repair the damage to his growing reputation. And if truth be told, it didn't really seem to hurt his standing with the fans that much. Now that he had come out from behind the scenes, so to speak, it wasn't just a case that he was appearing all over the media: he was required to appear in person, too. Something was needed to test the water, see how a tour should be planned and probe the extent of fan demand, and so a gig was announced in late August 2010 at the Bowery Ballroom in New York. Tickets sold out almost immediately, confirming that here was a bona fide new sensation and, in the event, the show was as successful as the single. Clearly enjoying himself and dressed in a natty blue tuxedo, white shirt and narrow black tie, as was his four-piece backup band, including Lawrence, who supplied vocals, one reviewer compared them to "the house act for some sixties sock hop". There were a lot of girls in the audience and a lot of screaming. Bruno looked like the cat that had got the cream.

This performance was in many ways as important as the single itself, because if Bruno wanted to have a long-term career as a performer, then it was imperative to show that he could actually perform. And he did. Within moments of him bounding on to the stage it was obvious that he had the prerequisite charisma, and with that he launched into songs from the forthcoming album. It combined humour in songs like 'Marry You', a hymn to weddings in Vegas ("who cares if we're trashed/I've got a fist full of cash") and poignancy in the ballad 'Grenade', all about unrequited love, which was to be Bruno's second single, of which more below. There was some dancing, some jiving and some hip-hop before Bruno closed the show and brought down the house with 'Just The Way You Are'.

Of course, it should have been no surprise that Bruno was an accomplished live performer – after all, he'd been doing it since the age of four. But no one in the wider world knew that and now Bruno was proving himself to a whole new audience and a whole new set of fans. And this was the proof that Bruno wasn't just going to be a performer: he was going to be a heartthrob, too. The reaction of the women present was testimony to that. For Bruno himself, this was some kind of rite of passage: he'd made it through from cute kid performer, to guy with a great future behind him on account of the dropped record label, to bona fide mainstream performer, and one who was starting to radiate sex appeal, at that. Part of it was self-fulfilling – success breeds confidence, which itself becomes extremely attractive – but Bruno was also showing that he had that elusive element that simply couldn't be manufactured – star quality. It really was all coming together now.

After the New York triumph, an appearance on *Saturday Night Live* ensued. Bruno wore the same outfit, clearly an homage to the sixties bands he had loved so much in his youth, but now the wider audience was taking to him, too. He was the musical guest on the show, and again, it was a careful introduction of Bruno to a wider audience: first it was the New York elite and now it was the rest of the States on prime-time television. He started with 'Just The Way You Are' and followed it with 'Grenade'. His performance, unlike so many before him, was flawless. Again, Bruno passed the test with flying colours; it became increasingly obvious that a major new star was born. And it was, according to the man himself, a long-term dream come true. Bruno was going from strength to strength.

But now the next challenge was to be: how to follow that first smash hit single? It was imperative that Bruno came up with another hit, and fast. And so it was that in September 2010, in the wake of the stunning success of 'Just The Way You Are', Bruno's next single, 'Grenade', was released. Initially a promotional single alongside 'Liquor Store Blues', it was then deemed to be strong enough to act as the next major release. As before, it was a Smeezingtons number, with additional writers brought in in the form of Brody Brown, Moe Faisal, Claude Kelly and Andrew Wyatt.

Its origins, however, lay in another song. "I was with my friend Benny Blanco [songwriter of hits like Katy Perry's 'I Kissed A Girl' and Ke$ha's 'TiK ToK'] and he was playing me some songs, and he played me this song that had a lyric like [the one in 'Grenade']... he said, this band is not signed, this is a CD that wasn't released," Bruno told Idolator.com. "I said to Benny, 'I can relate to that so much, I want to take that and make it my own'. He was in contact with the dude, and I started writing my version, basically. It's a heartbreaking, heartbreak song, and I think everyone can relate to that. You're so in love with this woman and you don't understand, 'What am I doing wrong? What am I not giving to you? I'll go as far as putting a bullet in my brain for you, and why can't I get that kind of love in return?'" Indeed, according to the song, he would catch a grenade for her – but she won't do the same.

Once the Smeezingtons got their hands on it, however, there was still plenty of work to be done. All three were perfectionists (which is one of the reasons they became so successful) and there was a good deal of to-ing and fro-ing before they were happy with the final result. The final line, in particular, "But you won't do the same," gave them a great deal of trouble, taking two months before they were finally happy with the result.

"'Grenade' took several months to write, regardless even of doing the actual production," Ari told soundonsound.com. "We had the first and second line of the chorus, and then we found the third line, and after that we had to figure out how to make the music change, write the verse and keep it interesting, and end it. That was months of sitting in the studio and losing sleep over how we were going to make the song work. We knew that we had something awesome, but we weren't always confident that it would work."

It is also telling that when the men were interviewed about how they put the song together, they would speak about it in very different ways. Bruno would talk about what the song conveyed, the emotion of it all, whereas Ari was far more concerned with the production side. Bruno talked about broken hearts and the pain of a girl who won't love you, Ari concentrated on what went on behind the scenes. "'Grenade' was definitely one of the more difficult songs on the album to write, but I wouldn't say any of them were easy," he continued. "They were all hard work! On top, 'Grenade' was initially produced in a different way. We had recorded the song with a more guitar-based arrangement that was 15bpm faster. Bruno played the song slower live, and the label was like, 'Oh, that's incredible.' So we had to reproduce it in the way you hear it now on the radio, two days before the album was supposed to be handed in.

"There was quite a bit of deadline stress involved in that. We completely rearranged and re-recorded the song, including the vocals. The drums in 'Grenade' came from a combination of my MPC and some software drums, and I created the piano sound in the Fantom. The rest of the synth sounds came from the Virus, and I use the V-synth and the MicroKorg on pretty much everything. Bruno and I played the keyboards and Brody Brown played the bass. He's an incredible musician who has a great feel and he can play everything. He played on a few tracks on the album, but he's not a member of the Smeezingtons." It was a pretty different take on it from Bruno's – but that, of course, is why they all worked together so well.

On the whole, the critics were pretty positive about it. "If you thought Bruno Mars was just about happy, cheerful pop songs, 'Grenade' is your wake-up call," wrote Bill Lamb on about. com. "He has been wronged, and now he's telling the tale. This immaculately constructed pop song takes its place among the great break-up songs. Bruno Mars cements his position as the top new artist of 2010."

Chapter 8

Doo-Wops & Hooligans

And so the moment came: the real test of whether Bruno was going to make it as a star. That moment was the release of his first album, *Doo-Wops & Hooligans*, and a great deal was at stake. The success of the first two singles was a huge relief, of course, but even so, there was still the chance of failure, even at this late stage. That could not be allowed to happen. Bruno had come too far, and the thought of the album performing badly was almost too much to bear.

The omens were good, however; the marketing machine had swung into motion and all looked set to succeed. Bruno was in actual fact a marketing man's dream: now that all the nonsense about whether he was black, Hispanic, Hawaiian, Filipino and the rest had been allowed to calm down, it was clear that what he actually was was an extremely photogenic and talented musician. Magazines were beginning to feature him on their covers and he was appearing all over the media now: he took to it as if to the manor born. Effortlessly cool, as often as not sporting shades and his trademark fedora, Bruno looked every inch the pop star. He was charismatic, too. And here the fact that he was just 5′5″ worked to his advantage, because the camera adds weight and stature and in Bruno's case that could only work to his advantage. Many pop stars are in fact surprisingly small – Mick Jagger being another who is much shorter than he looks on stage.

The 10 tracks on the album were: 'Grenade', 'Just The Way You Are', 'Our First Time', 'Runaway Baby', 'The Lazy Song', 'Marry You', 'Talking To The Moon', 'Liquor Store Blues' featuring Damian Marley, 'Count On Me' and 'The Other Side', featuring CeeLo Green and B.o.B. It was immediately obvious that Bruno had been influenced by a wide range of music: "And yet Mr. Mars is a true rarity," wrote Jon Caramanica in *The New York Times*. "His debut album, *Doo-Wops & Hooligans* (Elektra), which was released on Tuesday, is an effortless, fantastically polyglot record that shows him to be a careful study across a range of pop songcraft. 'Grenade' is a hybrid of ethereal eighties pop with modern-day Kanye Westesque drums. On the jumpy, salacious 'Runaway Baby', he channels Little Richard. 'The Lazy Song' and 'Liquor Store Blues' borrow heavily from roots reggae, and on 'Our First Time' Mr. Mars approximates the slinkiness of Sade." There were an awful lot of comparisons to Michael Jackson, especially with 'Grenade'.

The album was attracting a good deal of attention, not just because this brand new talent had appeared to spring out of nowhere and was taking the world of music by storm. For a start, the title was pretty unusual and as such, bound to make people take notice and sit up. "Pretty funky, huh?" Bruno told 4Music.com. "There's a lot of reasons for calling it *Doo-Wops & Hooligans*. It explains the two sides of me. Doo-wop is a special form of music I grew up on. It's straight to the point, very simple. I have songs like that. There are no tricks or mind-boggling lyrics. I have that simple, romantic side of me but I'm also just a young, regular dude and that's like the hooligan side! I think the album caters to men and women, doo–wops and hooligans! Boom! Quote me on that!"

They did. Bruno was an attractive figure: he had a certain air of cockiness about him, mixed in with vulnerability. It was perfectly possible to imagine him having a beer with the boys before romancing the girls: he had a universal appeal.

Jon Caramanica's review in *The New York Times* was unusually positive for a newcomer on the scene. Could it get any better? Yes. "With his sweet smile and aggressive talent, Mars is no shy flower," said Ken Tucker in npr.org. "He's positioning himself to become a new prince of pop – maybe even a king. *Doo-Wops & Hooligans* is such an impressive, varied and intense experience, it makes you wonder whether he can sustain it. These are some of the most pleasurable worries you can have about a new star; they're worries that, if they've even occurred to Bruno Mars, have been dismissed as he gets on with the work of creating more pleasure."

Of course, while this was Bruno's first album per se, he was in fact far more of a veteran of the industry than anyone had realised. Yes, he was going to have to sustain it, but the fact is that he already had done. A consistently high track record with the Smeezingtons meant that he had far more experience than the existence of just one album to date would seem to allow.

But the reviews continued to speak for themselves. "*Doo-Wops & Hooligans* aptly applies Mars' studio talents: instant-access melodies, creamy production, sly snatches of dance-floor swagger," wrote Leah Greenblatt in *Entertainment Weekly* (in the same review she also mentioned his drug arrest). "And he do, in his own postmillennial way, wop; a malt-hop heart beats beneath the digital skin of tracks like the buoyant 'Marry You' and woebegone 'Talking To The Moon'. Atmospheric opener 'Grenade' and 'Runaway Baby', with its sixties-soul snap, are immediate stylistic standouts, though other modes suit him less well; 'Our First Time' feels a bit too Al B. 'The Lazy Song' is perhaps better left to Jason Mraz. Still, *Hooligans* proves that this onetime background player makes a pretty solid first banana. B+." Not the highest of grades, but a pretty solid endorsement all the same.

It wasn't just the entertainment press: the serious dailies were covering it as well, remarking on the way on the fact that Bruno seemed to have sprung out of nowhere. "We can't be sure, but Bruno Mars might be an android," Sean Fennessey began, tongue-in-cheek in the *Washington Post*. "The Hawaii-born singer-songwriter-producer-pop terror was unleashed onto the world this year, like a future-sent cyborg come to swallow the *Billboard* charts whole... It's all happening so fast – who will stop this Terminator? We ask because *Doo-Wops & Hooligans* indicates that Mars (real name: Peter Hernandez), treacle though his songs may be, appears primed for a durable career. This is a short album, with just 10 songs, but it is effortlessly tuneful – the songs often sound as if they have been written on the spot, a quality that is both endearing and damning."

On the other side of the pond, critics were equally enthusiastic. "Hawaiian-born Bruno Mars had a hand in many of last year's biggest hits, including CeeLo Green's chart-topping 'Forget You'," wrote Tom Gockelen-Kozlowski in the *Daily Telegraph*. "For his own album, Mars has saved up a bundle of top-drawer melodies, making commercial success all but a certainty. What makes this a really exciting debut, however, is the Kanye West-style genre-bending on 'Grenade', 'The Other Side' and 'Our First Time', which joins the dots between between Michael Jackson and Bob Marley."

And on it went. Consequence of Sound's Kevin Barber called it "fulfilling [with] very few holes"; Bruno was "a fresh act with full confidence in his abilities in writing, producing, and performing." *Rolling Stone*'s Jody Rosen called it "the year's finest debut" whose tracks "deliver pleasure without pretension".

Not everyone was complimentary, however. Andy Gill of *The Independent* believed that the album "seeks too hard to display Mars' multifaceted talents". Q said "mostly, he has little to say". Tim Sendra of allmusic called it "an uneven debut ... [that] doesn't tap into his potential as a writer or a producer". Alexis Petridis of *The Guardian* wrote that "Bruno Mars' pop nous is spoiled by some unfortunate vegetable metaphors". Eric Henderson writing for *Slant Magazine* said it "manages to wear out its welcome about halfway through", calling it an attempt to "please just about everybody". Scott Kara of *The New Zealand Herald* said it could have had more of both titular elements to raise its "potency". Ken Capobianco of *The Boston Globe* was disappointed that the album lacked an autobiographical aspect. However, these were all niggles. What most people accepted was that they were watching the emergence of a major new star.

As all this was going on, Bruno's fellow Smeezingtons were watching with a mixture of astonishment and delight. There was certainly no jealousy from them. "It's like watching my good friend become amazingly famous and people chase him," Ari told the *Huffington Post*. "And that's what he wanted." Ari, of course, wanted nothing of the sort for himself, content to be the backroom boy, the magician behind the scenes, or the "sleeping partner" as Bruno once called him, but even he, by virtue of the Bruno connection, was finding the spotlight shining strongly upon him now. Bruno might have been the poster boy, but there was growing curiosity about all the Smeezingtons and how this relatively low-profile outfit had suddenly produced someone who was turning into the next big thing. Bruno was hot, but it was now safe to say that Philip and Ari were both warming up nicely, too.

Indeed, all the boys were talking excitedly about how the album came about. Ari, the techie and the backroom boy, was especially enthused by it all. 'The Other Side', he told *Sound On Sound*, was written to somebody else's track. "We redid the sounds and then added things on top of it," he said. "Then we found out that there were all these writers on the track, and we went OMG! In general, we find it easier to write songs to an existing track. We approach writing songs almost like remixes: anything can change at any point in time. There's nothing set in stone."

'Talking To The Moon', he continued, was his favourite song from the album. In the beginning they "only had the first verse and the horns, but we knew that it was great. We then had three different bridges and we spent a lot of time trying to find out which one was the best. Jeff Bhasker is a fantastic musician, and he helped write that track. I think we tried to arrange and produce this in four different ways, mostly trying to figure out what kind of drums to put on."

As for 'The Lazy Song', Ari said it "was a very tough song to write, even though it is so simple. That song began one day when we were hanging around the studio and hadn't written a song for a few days and we were kind of burnt out and didn't feel like working. We felt lazy. K'naan was in the studio with us, and the four of us suddenly came up with this idea. After that we had a really hard time getting the groove and the drums to sit right. Once you have one piece of the puzzle, like when you realise that a drum track is good, you can add other things in after that."

And of course Philip had his say, talking here about 'Marry You'. "When we were coming up with that song, we had this image of a slow-mo video in Vegas of a couple running, and she's in her gown and he's in his tux, the wedding party is behind them and everyone's raging," he told *American Songwriter*. "This sort of crazy, daring, wedding feeling. It was more of a racy kind of idea, as opposed to this classic marriage tune it has become."

Bruno was managing to mix some fun into his schedule as well. On the one hand it was pretty much full-on – his moment had come and no one was going to waste it – but on the other he managed to find time to party as well, without ending up on a drugs charge. A fleeting visit to the UK to showcase some new material at the Notting Hill Arts Club also provided the opportunity to visit the nightclub Chinawhite in the company of Sugababe Amelle Berrabah, where the chanteuse raised eyebrows by running up a £15,000 bar bill. It was Amelle who was the centre of attention on that occasion, however, with security guards having to rescue her from the crush of fans.

The gig, which took place on the weekly YoYo night, went down well, however, and gave a foretaste of Bruno's easy-going relationship with his audience. Bounding on stage with Philip Lawrence and the rest of the band after a lively performance by Mike Posner, Bruno opened with 'Other Side', only to find that the microphone wasn't working properly. It could have spoiled the performance, but with some considerable charm, Bruno got the sound engineer to solve the problem, after which he set about wooing the crowd. They loved him as he moved on to 'Nothin' On You', before asking them, "I've always dreamed of performing Hendrix in London, can I play some Hendrix?" He could indeed, and with that it was Jimi Hendrix's 'Fire', followed by 'Billionaire'. He closed with 'Just The Way You Are'.

It was a short gig in a small club, but it was an important testing of the waters in the UK. The YoYo slot, held on Thursday nights, was a time when lesser known and untested talent got to show their stuff, and the audience reaction tended to be a good indication of whether any particular act had legs. It tended to be a pretty informed audience, too, made up not just of London's coolest customers, but also music industry insiders, keen to spot the next up-and-coming trend. They certainly found it in Bruno that night, not least because although two of the songs he performed were actually known as being the work of Travie McCoy and B.o.B., Bruno performed them every bit as well as the originals. At this transitional stage in his career, the music industry and the public was still not entirely sure to make of him – backstage technician eager for the limelight or up-and-coming star in his own right? – but this was proof that a major new talent was emerging onto the scene. It was also a taste of what was to come, for Bruno was to take on a much larger-scale tour shortly. And he needed people to know who he was.

He needed to prove that he could perform live, too. Despite his many years of experience, Bruno now had to be able to hold the stage as a charismatic adult performer and a smaller-scale gig, albeit in front of a very influential audience, was exactly the right way to test the waters. It was reassuring for Bruno's record bosses, too: they could see that he was an extremely charming, easy-going performer who effortlessly managed to hold the crowd. Bruno's Hawaiian background had a lot to do with this: he might have been resident in frenetic LA by this time, but that background of surf and the Pacific gave Bruno a laid-back charm that clearly rocked the crowd.

Which is not to say that he was not an energetic performer – he was. His performance was characterised by the odd pelvic thrust – he was a young man, eager to please, after all, and all those years impersonating Elvis had left their mark – and he was clearly extremely musical in his ability to dance, as well. This was in the run-up to the release of the first single, and this and similar performances had put Bruno in such demand that he had to bring its release forward as fans were so keen to play it that they were downloading covers of it, but such travails were considerably better than having garnered no interest at all. A part of Bruno still couldn't believe that all this was happening, that it was finally and so spectacularly coming together at last, but it was. And he was loving every moment along the way.

His recent collaborators didn't always know what to think about what was happening either. In an interview with *The Guardian*, in which he was compared to James Bond, with Bruno as the technical specialist Q, CeeLo Green, with whom Bruno had performed 'Fuck You' (the title was changed to 'Forget You' for the radio broadcast) sounded somewhat wry on the subject of their recent hit. "It wouldn't work for just anyone," he said. "Some people have misconstrued Bruno's contribution as him writing the song for me. If he knew the song was gonna be a big hit, he'd-a wrote it for himself! Nobody else would've got away with it but me. Look at me! I'm not ideal image-wise, I don't think. I get a chance to stand out there and redefine what's doable. I am a fuck you – that's why the song works." It was also an acknowledgement that Bruno was himself now a sharply rising star.

Bruno was sparking some personal interest as well. He confided in one newspaper that he was in a relationship (with Rita), but added that he was a bit of a Casanova, a hint perhaps that this one was not going to last. Meanwhile, he was enjoying an aspect of stardom he had not had so much in the past, the ability to travel and see something of the world. This was London, after all, possibly the world capital of pop music. And Bruno was making it his own. Meanwhile his growing influence on the music industry was underlined by the fact that in Britain, on that autumn's series of *The X Factor*, one of its more talented competitors, Matt Cardle, had performed Bruno's hit 'Just The Way You Are'. A few months previously, few people had even heard of Bruno. Now he was being covered on one of television's most popular shows.

Of course, Bruno was not alone in having started as a writer for other people before moving on to become a star in his own right. Lady Gaga was the best known of the new breed, having written for several household names before turning into a global sensation herself, and there were many who pointed out that in today's risk-averse music industry, it was a way of trying out a new artist before making a final commitment. David Miller,

vice-president of international marketing for Atlantic Records –
Bruno's label – agreed with that. "It's a dilemma for our labels,"
he told *The Guardian*. "You want success. It's difficult to commit
to finance for new artists. He [Bruno] has a team around him
that's experienced and know the industry fairly well. I certainly
do think that once you've been in it and written a couple of songs
and worked with other artists, you do get that opportunity to
kind of grow slowly from nothing to something."

Bruno wasn't the only one enjoying this, of course. His band
was aptly named the Hooligans and the initial line-up consisted of
Bruno, Philip, Phredley Brown, Jamareo Artis, Eric Hernandez
(Bruno's brother), Kameron Whalum, Dwayne Dugger, James
King and Kenji Chan, who was to leave in 2012. That same year
John Fossit joined. Eric, born in 1976, was a few years older than
his little brother, but had similarly grown up immersed in music
and was now playing the drums. (Eric had also had a nickname
growing up, E-Panda, which he still occasionally used, such as
on his Facebook page, but unlike Bruno's, it was never used
professionally.)

The band were certainly set to be active that autumn. Apart
from one-off gigs, such as those at the Bowery Ballroom and
the Notting Hill Arts Club, Bruno was to embark on not one
but three tours before the end of the year. The first was as a
supporting act to Maroon 5 and the second supporting One
Republic and Travie McCoy: Bruno supported the former across
the States in the first half of October and the latter across Europe
in the second half of October and a few dates in November.
He was going to need every ounce of his stamina, however,
because just a few weeks later, he was going to kick off his
own *Doo-Wops & Hooligans* tour, starting in San Francisco and
ending up, appropriately enough, in Hawaii. Most of the dates
sold out shortly after they were announced and with Bruno's
debut single now surpassing the two million sales mark, it didn't

look as if the Bruno bandwagon was going to grind to a halt any time soon.

Nor was that all. In the run-up to Christmas, Bruno was to be putting in some heavy promotional work, including appearances at KISSFM's Jingle Ball at Los Angeles' Nokia Theatre on December 5, Q102's Jingle Ball at Camden, NJ's Susquehanna Bank Center on December 8, Z100's Jingle Ball at New York's world famous Madison Square Garden on December 10, and 93.3 FLZ's Jingle Ball at Tampa's St. Pete Times Forum on December 12.

Towards the end of the year, the rewards proper started to flow in. Both Bruno and the Smeezingtons were nominated for a plethora of Grammys: Bruno, sometimes alone and sometimes with the others, was up for Best Rap Song and Best Rap Song/ Sung Collaboration for 'Nothin' On You', Record of the Year for 'Nothin' On You' and 'Fuck You', Song of the Year for 'Fuck You', Producer of the Year, Non-Classical and Best Male Pop Vocal Performance, the last of which he actually won, beating such luminaries as Michael Bublé and Michael Jackson, which must have felt particularly sweet. That year, only Eminem weighed in with more nominations, namely 10 to Bruno's seven. It was also now that 'Grenade' started soaring up the charts, adding yet more lustre to Bruno's star. Newspapers were now calling Bruno the "Honolulu hunk". He had certainly made heartthrob grade, as the increasing number of screaming fans testified.

Even so, the sheer speed with which he had shot from zero to hero was still taking many people aback. Come January and he was back in London, now playing a gig at the Café de Paris, a considerably bigger and more prestigious venture than the Notting Hill Arts Club. It elicited a curious review from Caroline Sullivan in *The Guardian*, which was very complimentary yet underlined the slightly curious position in which Bruno now found himself. On the one hand he was very famous – but on the other he was still breaking through. "The Hawaiian-born vocalist/ producer is a skilled creator of singable melodies, as witnessed by his contribution to hits last year by B.o.B and Travie McCoy," she wrote. "He sang both tonight - B.o.B.'s 'Nothin' On You' and McCoy's 'Billionaire' – and only the stoniest of hearts could have denied their breezy charm, especially when filtered through Mars' sweet, soulful voice. Yet there's a lot of right-place-right-time about his success, because while he may be a highly capable musician, he's not a star... It was obvious that Mars is one of that dying breed: a journeyman who honed his craft in local bars and can still switch between R&B, rock and doo-wop (hence the title of his album, *Doo-Wops & Hooligans*) as required."

But Bruno was well on his way to becoming a star and other reviewers recognised this. "The fanfare from *Also Sprach Zarathustra* is a big opening gambit, at once cheesily over familiar (from 2001: *A Space Odyssey* and a thousand sporting broadcasts) yet still promising spectacle and glory," wrote Neil McCormick in the *Daily Telegraph*. "Bounding energetically on stage in a sharp, black suit and tie, flashing his choppers like a dental model and swinging a Stratocaster, Bruno Mars is clearly not short of confidence. On his London debut, the Hawaiian-born, LA-based singer-songwriter delivered an almost ludicrously entertaining set with all the pizzazz of a veteran showman. Mars is man of the moment, number one in the single and album charts. With his black pompadour and boyishly handsome Latino looks, he comes across like an old-fashioned pop idol, from long before Simon Cowell annexed the concept."

High praise indeed, but McCormick was spot on. Bruno was in an excellent mood: both 'Grenade' and *Doo-Wops & Hooligans* were topping their respective charts and he was clearly out to have a good time. Wearing what was becoming a signature look of natty suit and tie, hair slicked back and looking every inch the polished, professional entertainer he was born to be, Bruno bombarded his audience with all the charm and energy he'd displayed at the Notting Hill Arts Club, belting out songs such as 'The Other Side', 'Top Of The World', 'Money (That's All I Want)' and 'Billionaire'. Then Bruno infused his act with the same cheeky chappy banter he'd displayed before: "Can we just have fun for two minutes?" he inquired. Yes, was the answer, and so Bruno launched into Nirvana's 'Smells Like Teen Spirit' using the lyrics of Billie Jean. Not everyone could have carried that one off but he managed it. Then it was on to 'Marry You', 'The Lazy Song', 'Count On Me', 'Nothin' On You' and 'Grenade', to which the audience, clearly having the time of their lives, sang along. That would have been that but the audience demanded an encore and so Bruno returned to the stage for 'Talking To The Moon' and a reprise of 'The Other Side'. The crowd loved it. Bruno's popularity in the UK was coming to resemble that on the other side of the pond.

A review in *The Independent* summed it up perfectly. "The holders of the hottest ticket in town are mostly industry types, but make no mistake: when this guy goes on tour properly, there'll be hysteria," wrote Simon Price. "When he says 'It wasn't so long since we were playing bars and clubs', it's with the humility of a man who knows he'll never need to do that again. His stock in trade is bustling funk-pop, smooth soul-rock and light acoustic reggae. He's Mike Posner meets Orson meets Maroon 5 meets Jack Johnson meets Mark Ronson. It's all mainstream fare, tailor made to be heard at low volume on the nation's office radios. A bit of Mars a day helps Britain work, rest and play. It doesn't hurt that he's a looker. Mars only has to say the word 'ladies' in his smoky voice for the ambient crowd noise suddenly to leap as many octaves as decibels. He also has a relaxed charm that you wouldn't necessarily expect from a man who has a potential prison sentence hanging over him for a Las Vegas cocaine bust."

Ouch! Because that drugs trial was indeed still hanging over his head. Put in the context of all that growing success on both sides of the Atlantic, it becomes clear quite how much Bruno was risking on that reckless night. But in his (and his lawyers') attempts to deal with the situation, he wasn't putting a foot wrong. Bruno just had to play on as if nothing had happened and nothing was wrong and that's exactly what he was doing. And he was gaining a lot of respect from many quarters by dealing with a very difficult situation well.

Bruno had, of course, made his first waves in the industry by writing for other people and in the wake of all this solo success, people were by now absolutely queuing up to try to get him on board. Under headlines such as Going To Mars, Life On Mars and any other puns they could come up with, newspapers and magazines excitedly revealed that the likes of Alexandra Burke, R&B star Ne-Yo and JLS were all hoping to work with him – and indeed, Ne-Yo had already done so. "I worked with Bruno before my name was even Ne-Yo," he told the *Daily Star*. "We have been talking about doing something together again. I don't want to give too much away, but it's being talked about. To see him doing so well and come out with these big tunes for himself makes me so proud." It was making an awful lot of people proud – and rich. Bruno was going to be reaping the rewards of all this in many different ways.

In February 2011, the Grammy finally came round. Bruno allowed himself a small moment of satisfaction: success, now that it had finally arrived, was sweet. "For me it is an 'I told you so'," he added in the *Daily Star* interview. "I told you I can do it and I told you I can write a song for the world. For a long time, people stopped believing in me or had their doubts about me. I never signed up for this to be famous, all I know to do is music. So that's what I want to do. That these songs are working is justice for me." In other words, the doubters deserved to hear a "Who's sorry now."

That month Bruno won his first Grammy. The music industry might have been slow to cotton on to his talent, but it was making up for it now. But the award was more than just for Bruno's work: it marked the massive change that had taken place in Bruno's life over the past year. He really was a bona fide star.

Chapter 9

The Flyin' Hawaiian

By this time, Bruno was becoming not only a famous singer, but a veteran of the chat show circuit. He had made appearances on ABC's *The View*, NBC's *The Tonight Show With Jay Leno* and *Late Night With Jimmy Fallon*, VH1's *Do Something Awards*, TBS' *Lopez Tonight*, and Fox's 2010 *Teen Choice Awards*. As his face grew increasingly familiar to television viewers, he began to make the next transition in his journey, from star to household name. Then on February 13, 2011, Bruno finally received the official acclaim that was his due. That was the night of the Grammy awards for which Bruno had received six nominations: in the event he walked away with Best Male Pop Vocal Performance. The transition had been made. Whatever was to happen next in his career, Bruno was now part of pop music history and there would be no going back after this.

The touring by now was continuous. Shortly after the Grammys, Bruno was back in the UK: his sheer scope and range continued to take audiences by surprise. "His musical dexterity showed no bounds, having started proceedings with his very own drum solo before taking centre stage vocally," wrote Dave Esson in the *Sunday Express* in a review of a concert in Glasgow. "He can deliver easy on the ear reggae in 'The Lazy Song', strumalong Jack Johnson-like with 'Marry You' or machine-gun Motown on 'Runaway Baby' (accompanied by natty James Brown dancing – was there no end to this boy's talents?) and to be honest, the crowd would have let him read the phone book while playing a banjo as long as they could take a picture with the hundreds of mobile phones thrust in the Sauchiehall Street air throughout." Meanwhile, in other concerts, such as one staged soon afterwards by Eliza Doolittle, artists were now singing cover versions of Bruno's songs, in her case 'Grenade'.

Unusually, in an industry that is often considered to be so cutthroat, his peers didn't have a bad word to say about him. In April 2011, Bruno made the *Time* 100 list of the most influential people in the world, and none other than his old friend and collaborator B.o.B wrote the accompanying text. And he couldn't have been more complimentary if he'd tried. "There are a lot of people in this world who can sing and play the piano and guitar," he wrote. "Hell, I sing and play the piano and guitar. But there's something different about Bruno Mars. He has a musicality, a presence in his voice that I've never heard from anyone else. Bruno, 25, is part of this new wave of musicians who can do everything: sing, play, write, produce. When he performs live, nothing is prerecorded or fudged. It's a straight-up, classic performance. That's so rare these days."

As his audiences continued to show blind adoration for him, it could get a little tricky at times. Fans were now beginning to hurl fake grenades onto the stage, which was actually somewhat nerve racking for the performers up there. "Since I've been singing 'Grenade' I've been getting more fake ones thrown at me," he told the *Daily Star*. "At first it was cute now it's beginning to spook my band out. With the stage lights on you can't see anything. It's dangerous and scares the sh★t out of me. I don't mind a few bras.

They're better than candy. That can really hurt." Such was the price of fame. It had an upside, too, as Bruno admitted elsewhere, saying he used it to attract women. "Why be famous if you can't go, 'Excuse me, I don't know if you know me but I am a big deal – I am the 'Grenade' guy'?" he asked. Why indeed? He clearly had lost none of his liking for a pretty face.

Awards continued to beckon: Bruno was nominated for four gongs at the MTV Europe music awards and won Best International Artist at the BT Digital Music Awards. In the autumn of that year it was time for another collaboration, this time with Bad Meets Evil, aka the hip-hop duo Royce da 5´9˝ and Eminem. The song was called 'Lighters' and made liberal use of profanities, which was commented upon in some quarters. "Bruno Mars wants us to chase our dreams," said pluggedin.com. "And Bad Meets Evil rap duo Eminem and Royce da 5´9˝ (who first collaborated more than a decade ago) are more than willing to tell us how they chased theirs. The difference? These two Detroit rappers use a lot more nasty words to get the job done than guest contributor Mars does on this Top 20 hit from Bad Meets Evil's chart-topping album, *Hell: The Sequel*."

It received mixed critical reviews, ironically in some cases because of Bruno's involvement. Rob Markman from MTV News said, "It's hard to imagine a time when Eminem wasn't regarded as one of rap's elite, but his past drug abuse did take its toll before he reemerged triumphant on last year's Grammy Award-winning album 'Recovery'… The gritty Detroit MC [Royce] recalls his own battles to the top, referencing doubters at every turn." *Billboard* editor Jason Lipshutz thought that the song did not fit in with the rest of *Hell: The Sequel*, but liked it anyway: "[The] track doesn't fit with EP, but Em's effortless confidence carries the celebratory anthem." Jon Dolan of *Rolling Stone* said, "All the evil meeting badness can get pretty ugly […] But there's genuine humanity, too." Magazine *XXL* felt it was "another break from the typical vicious lyrical assault". About.com's Bill Lamb found it "an engaging, soulful pop hip-hop blend".

But not everyone was keen. David Jeffries from Allmusic said that "The glossy 'Lighters' feels more like a Bruno Mars track than Detroit diesel," which was a point in its favour in the eyes of many people, but clearly not absolutely everyone. Consequence of Sound was another naysayer: Winston Robbins said the chorus, by Bruno, does not fit into a rap song and would have done better on a solo track or with another artist, "but it is so far from home next to the hard verses of two of rap's bad boys". Chad Grischow of IGN said it was "strange" and "unusual". "In the end, this brief look at the duo's skills does not fully deliver what you expect, but still leaves you wanting to hear more."

PopMatters said: "It's easy to press the skip button if you'd like to." Web magazine pluggedin.com liked Bruno's input, but not his colleagues'. Royce da 5′9″ stated somewhat coolly, "I don't want that audience to think that I can only do one thing. It shows versatility on my end and it was a good way to set up [supergroup] Slaughterhouse."

Not that Bruno needed to be unduly concerned by any of this. In September that year it was announced that Bruno's single 'It Will Rain' was going to be featured on the soundtrack of *Twilight Saga: Breaking Dawn – Part 1*, thus linking him to one of the most popular and successful film franchises of all time. The song was another success, going to the top of the *Billboard* charts. It was a typical Bruno/Smeezingtons production, a love ballad with an accompanying video that intertwined shots of Bruno and a girlfriend with footage from *Breaking Dawn: Part 1*. The *Rolling Stone* review, written by Simon Vozick-Levinson, summed up the neat synchronicity between these two cultural phenomena: "Who better than Bruno Mars to lead the promotional blitz for *Twilight*'s latest soundtrack?" he wrote. "Mars' clean-cut looks and gently scuffed croon make him an ideal nonthreatening crush

– and last year's smash 'Grenade', on which he threatened to blow himself up for attention, proved his knack for overheated romantic dialogue. Mars gets similarly melodramatic on this ballad ('If you ever leave me, baby, leave some morphine at my door'), but the real point is the song's desperately yearning melody." Bruno was becoming very well known for those.

His next single, 'Runaway Baby', which Bruno performed on the UK's *The X Factor*'s results show on October 30, 2011, didn't do quite so well, but it, too, featured on a film, in this case *Friends With Benefits*. It was also to feature in a future movie, *Escape From Planet Earth* in 2013. Any negative reviews might also have been deemed pretty insignificant in the wake of another raft of Grammy nominations: six in total, comprising Album of the Year and Best Pop Vocal Album for *Doo-Wops & Hooligans*, Record of the Year, Song of the Year and Best Pop Solo Performance for 'Grenade', and Producer of the Year, Non-Classical at the 54th Grammy Awards (although in the event he didn't actually win any of them).

As the touring continued, Bruno continued to charm. At the MTV EMAs afterparty, he was pictured bumping and grinding with Wynter Gordon, before delighting everyone by taking to the piano. There was a rumoured romance with Amelle Berrabah of the Sugababes – "She's absolutely smitten with him and keeps saying he's the one," said a friend of Amelle's to the *Daily Star*. "It's getting very serious very fast. Who knows what will happen next? None of us would be surprised if they got engaged. He smashed it on *The X Factor*. His career is going from strength to strength and he's fast becoming an international superstar. We just hope he'll have the time to treat her right – she can't get her heart broken again." In the event, Bruno was to end up with someone different, but he continued to attract women wherever he went, even confiding what music he played during intimate moments. It was 'Eye Of The Tiger' by Survivor, 'Macho Man' by the Village People and 'My Heart Will Go On' by Celine Dion, although it was hard to escape the conclusion that those choices were not just a little tongue in cheek.

He also continued to win awards, next being named Best Pop Male at the American Music Awards, along with being crowned King of Playlist's music poll (Lady Gaga was Queen). He even came to the attention of Britain's Prime Minister, David Cameron, admittedly not in a very complimentary way, when the latter referred to his children's appalling taste in music, including, apparently, Bruno. He was now famous enough to make the news even when it didn't actually involve him – in early 2012, the actress Demi Moore was rushed to hospital in the wake of the breakdown of her marriage to Ashton Kutcher. It was soon reported that Ashton had been given the news while attending one of Bruno's concerts in Brazil. He was then mentioned in a very different context when the rapper K'Naan expressed anger over the fact that his song 'Wavin' Flag' had been used by Republican presidential candidate Mitt Romney during a Florida primary victory speech. This had, of course, been co-written and co-produced with Bruno and the Smeezingtons.

Bruno was also part of a group of artists who were said to be having a real effect on the music scene: 2011 was the first year for seven years in which pop albums sold more than rock albums, with Bruno, Lady Gaga, Jessie J and Adele responsible for seven of the BPI's Official Top Ten Albums. He also had the two top-selling songs of 2011, 'Just The Way You Are' and 'Grenade', and scored yet another triumph, this time in Britain, when he walked off with the award for Best International Male at the Brits. To celebrate the occasion, Bruno took over the Warner Music boat, complete with a 30-strong entourage, who he took to the Warner party afterwards. Will Hodgkinson of *The Times* was present and wrote afterwards that one of the things he'd learned at the awards is that male pop stars are tiny: "Bruno Mars is a perfectly proportioned miniature man," he said. "His hair and his stack heels give a bit of a boost but otherwise he's a Fun Size Mars Bar: just like the real thing but smaller." But he was the real thing, and then some. He had turned into the man women wanted to be with and other men wanted to be. Bruno was living the dream and loving every moment along the way. And that twinkle in his eye continued to twinkle, as he noticed the new girl band Stooshe at the awards: "He came to our table at the BRITs afterparty and was dancing around it with us," said Stooshe member Karis Anderson. "He was lovely, introducing us to everyone and partying the night away. He remembered us from Wireless festival last year so hopefully we can do more with him."

He still wasn't taking himself too seriously, however. Bruno's quiff had been quite the talking point: according to the man himself, he maintained his look as follows: "I call my hairstyle the Wamp And Stomp," he said "I can't give you exact measures but it's a lot of margarine, natural fruit juices and berries and, surprisingly, barbecue potato Popchips. It stays in place for a while after that." Presumably, this was a joke.

However, there was a big downside to celebrity and that is that it almost invariably attracts lawsuits. Bruno was no exception to the rule, although in his case it was he who had set out a lawsuit rather than being on the receiving end of one. From some time in 2011, this had been rumbling on in the background: Bruno had filed a suit against Bug Music, Inc. for violating the stipulations of his contract. According to documents from the Los Angeles County Superior Court Bug Music was refusing to let Bruno out of his contract, even though Bruno claimed he had completed the requirements of his contract. Of course, Bruno's circumstances had changed dramatically since he'd signed that contract and everything to do with him was big business. He had by now sold 36 million albums around the world. It was hardly surprising that Bug wanted to keep him on board. According to Bruno's contract, the company required him to deliver a set amount of music before he could terminate his contract. Following the completion of this stipulation, Bug had a specific period of time during which they could offer to renew their contract with him.

According to Bruno, he had delivered Bug the required amount of music by February 2011, but the company failed to renew his contract within the time limit, thus ending his contract on May 12. Bug claimed, however, that Bruno Mars had yet to complete his assigned contract, which gave them access to 50 per cent of the copyrights to his music.

Matters appeared to be resolved when Bug, which also had Ari Levine on its books, was acquired by BMG Chrysalis' parent BMG Rights Management last September in a deal reported to be worth $30 million. Ari remained with BMG Chrysalis. It was the outcome everyone wanted: BMG CEO Hartwig Masuch said: "We are thrilled that Bruno Mars – one of contemporary music's most creative and prolific songwriters – has joined the BMG roster. His decision to sign with us reflects our commitment to make BMG a home for the best music talent in the world." And BMG North America executive vice president Richard Blackstone added: "In such a short time, Bruno Mars has created a tremendous footprint in the musical world. Whether he's writing for himself or others, he creates magic and there is simply no limit to where his talent can take him."

Of course, this was the kind of success Bruno could only have dreamed of until comparatively recently: he was being fought over by major figures in the music industry. He was now well off enough to pay millions for a house befitting a pop star in LA's Laurel Canyon area, of which more anon, and there were rumours that the producers of *The X Factor* were trying to get him on the show as a judge. And that was not the only area in which he was in demand. One day, while eating at the Co-op restaurant in New York's Hotel on Rivington, Bruno spotted a beautiful, vivacious woman chatting animatedly at a nearby table. Bruno was not shy when it came to approaching women he found attractive. Within a very short time the two became an item and soon afterwards, one of show business's hottest celebrity couples.

★ ★ ★

Jessica Marie Caban was born on June 13, 1982, making her three years older than Bruno, of Puerto Rican extraction, and brought up in New York's Bronx district. She became a model, dancer and actress, kicking off her career in 2002 when she was chosen by Jennifer Lopez to represent New York in her Nationwide Model Search for her clothing line JLo. She didn't win, ending as runner-up, but this was enough to get her noticed and she landed a page in *YM* magazine as the beauty opener for the 2002 issue. The following year she won a print campaign for Clean & Clear and her career was effectively launched.

Jessica, who incidentally at 5′4″ is an inch shorter than Bruno, began making her way up through the ranks of the celebrity world. In 2004, she launched a television career, acting as a host on Viva America and a big range of activities followed, including stints on magazines, commercials and television shows such as *Law & Order*. In 2008 she won Model Latina, which landed her a turn with Q Management, and her film debut followed in 2010 with *Shades Of Love*, for which she won Best Actress at the Boston International Film Festival and Hoboken International Film Festival. She is also a model for Steve Madden Clothing, Coog.com and Ideeli.com. Jessica's hobbies were travelling, reading (Stephen King was a favourite), hanging out with family and friends: "There's a lot more to me than what you see... I come from a rough background but I always believed I can do anything I wanted. I'm lucky to have my parents' love and support. I get to do what I love and for that I am HAPPY and BLESSED!" she once said.

The first time the couple was ever actually seen together was, fittingly enough, via the medium of one of Bruno's videos. Big international star as he then was, Bruno was still more than capable of laughing at himself, as he showed in a Funny Or Die sketch: Funny Or Die was a comedy video website founded by Will Ferrell and Adam McKay's production company Gary Sanchez Productions. It contains exclusive material from some very famous names indeed, including Charlie Sheen, Patrick Stewart, Mila Kunis, Jim Carrey and Jerry Seinfeld, and now Bruno was about to join their ranks. The idea was that members of the site would vote on the videos, with the options 'funny' or 'die'.

So, it was high stakes and a lot to aim for. Bruno was seen cavorting to the soundtrack of Salt-N-Pepa's number 'Whatta Man': fans were treated to, amongst much else, seeing him skipping around in gold lamé shorts, alongside sending himself up in the guise of secret agent, paper towel mascot and kung fu master. All of these were superheroes: in the sketch, Bruno saved pregnant women, dogs and goldfish from burning buildings, also appeared as a ninja and a cowboy and literally broke off one man's arm. Alongside him at one point was a very pretty woman – Jessica, although she was by no means the only beauty featured, another being the Bollywood star Mallika Sherawat. But Jessica was the one who produced a real gleam in Bruno's eye. Regular Bruno watchers began to spot her rather more frequently after that.

Quite apart from heralding the start of a new and important relationship, the appearance on Funny Or Die also signalled the start of another new phase in Bruno's career. To make it in the longer term, Bruno had to become more than a singer – he had to become part of the whole fabric of the US and global entertainment industry and to do that he had to branch out. Appearing on a popular website and showing the ability to laugh at himself was one obvious way to go about that, but in the autumn of 2012, Bruno went a step further when he appeared as a guest host on *Saturday Night Live*. *SNL* as it is habitually known, is a US institution: running since 1975 and under its current name since 1980, it is a late-night comedy and variety show, which has launched some truly stellar careers. Dan Aykroyd, John Belushi, Chevy Chase, Gilda Radner and George Coe were all among its original cast members, while later performers included Eddie Murphy, Adam Sandler, Mike Myers and Chris Farley. In other words, the stakes were extremely high. This was a very high-profile gig, but failure could have been mortifying. Bruno had appeared on the show in the past as a performer, but he had never been called upon to carry the whole thing alone. He was also only the eighth musician ever to have been asked to do so, and given that the previous line-up included Elton John, Mick Jagger and Justin Timberlake, he was joining a very special elite indeed.

In the event, it was a spectacular success. Bruno pulled in the highest viewing figures for seven months, with the show opening with a spoof of that week's debate between President Obama and rival Mitt Romney. Drawing on his training of old, Bruno himself did impressions of Justin Bieber, Michael Jackson, Katy Perry, Aerosmith and Green Day in a skit about playing an intern at Pandora Headquarters as different stations were going down; he had, after all, done this sort of thing before.

By common consent, even though he had a few frozen moments, Bruno carried it off pretty well. "Bruno Mars… unlike almost all of these prior [musical] hosts, stated that he has never done comedy or acting before," said Pastemagazine.com. "At times, this really showed, as Mars could be incredibly stiff and uncomfortable, but other times he pulled off his duties. While this episode had a few sketches that were pretty terrible, it probably had the most laugh-out-loud moments of any episode so far this season."

Tara Fowler on popwatch was also won round. "Bruno Mars told us he was no comedian, but he was game for a surprisingly entertaining episode of *Saturday Night Live*. Was he of Justin Timberlake calibre? No, but who is?" she wrote (in fairness, Timberlake had always been more of a performer than a singer). "Mars was initially restricted to a lot of song numbers, which had me concerned. Still, the musical sketches were pretty funny, particularly one featuring Pandora, as you'll see below. Thankfully, after the Pandora one, Mars mostly kept the singing to his duties as musical guest and turned up the charm as a sad mouse, a one-eyed hotel employee and a fake ID maker. I had my doubts about you as a host, Mars, but you showed me wrong. I'd like to see you back someday!"

Rolling Stone took pretty much the same line. "Bruno was no slouch – it seems that Hawaiian performers, much like their pizza, come heaped with ham," it said. "He played to his strengths, singing an original song in the monologue; caricaturing Billie Joe Armstrong's snotty singing and rapping like Justin Bieber later; acting like a 17-year-old girl and dropping it like a hot pocket, before that. (It's either surprising or not-surprising that Bruno could pull that last one off so well.) Of course, Bruno took the night with his live performances…"

What was most noteworthy, however, was Bruno's sheer good naturedness in taking on the show. He might have been nervous and that might have showed a little, but he was prepared to try something new, experiment a little and show that he was ready for the wider world of show business along with his mainstream singing career. And besides, a little Hawaiian charm could go a very long way.

Chapter 10

Unorthodox Jukebox

As 2012 drew on, it was getting near the time for the release of that all-important second album. It is widely acknowledged that in many cases this can actually be more difficult than the first – when an artist first produces an album, it is often the product of what he or she has been working on for years and all their ideas and creativity has gone into it. A second album, on the other hand, needs to be produced an awful lot faster, if the artist is going to capitalise on their success and anyway, what if all the ideas went into the first one and there weren't any left? It is often with the second album, not the first, that an artist is called upon to prove that they have what it takes and so it was to be with Bruno now. Although he'd already come so far, so fast, his reputation still depended on the strength of one album and some singles, albeit exceedingly successful ones, alongside increasingly polished live performances. But he was going to have to prove himself again if he was really going to be in it for the long haul.

And so it was announced that *Unorthodox Jukebox* would be the second horse out of the Mars stables, as it were, while the first single, to be released a couple of months before the album itself, would be 'Locked Out Of Heaven'. It was the usual Smeezingtons line-up, with additional producers Mark Ronson, Jeff Bhasker and Emile Haynie. Heavily influenced by the Police, it was a new wave, funk and reggae song about the happiness brought on by a good relationship with great sex. Was it a coincidence that Bruno and Jessica were now solidly ensconced together? Almost certainly not.

Like so much that was now part of Bruno's life, a great deal hinged on those he had met when they were all making their way up in the world and now were having very fruitful working relationships with. One of these people was Jeff Bhasker, who had been born and raised in New Mexico and studied at Boston's Berklee College of Music. He started by "just playing keyboard gigs around Boston, like at weddings", he told americansongwriter.com, before working with the band Tavares and going to New York to seek fame and fortune, somewhat unfortunately arriving on September 11, 2001, the day of the terrible terrorist atrocity that stunned and appalled the rest of the world. Jeff went on to join a band called Lettuce, and started to have a small degree of success – "Once I got to New York, I got more into writing songs and recording my own voice," he said – and started working with an indie artist called Goapele, and from there with a mainstream act, rapper the Game. This was in 2005, and at about the same time he met a young artist, struggling to be heard. His name? Bruno Mars.

Like Bruno, Jeff was a struggling artist who was to learn through trial and error. "The first time I met Bruno, Mike Lynn put us together as an experiment and we kind of honed our songwriting craft together," said Jeff, adding that the well-known songwriter Steve Lindsey showed the two of them the techniques of writing pop music. "He'd mentor us, and kind of give us lectures as to what a hit pop song is, because you can have talent and music ability, but understanding what makes a hit pop song is a whole other discipline."

One of the most important things that he learned was that the most successful pop music is very cheerful. "The trick is to put your emotion into it while keeping it upbeat," he explained. "My first hit was Alicia Keys' 'Try Sleeping With A Broken Heart', and it's a sad song but the chorus says 'Tonight I'm gonna find a way to make it without you', so it's little things like that. Music and pop songs should have a positive message; there's a power in music to heal people and give them a good feeling. From the greatest songs like 'Let It Be' or 'Imagine' or 'Man In The Mirror', it's always about spinning something in a positive way. That's been an important thing for me." It was a lesson Bruno had also taken on board – he, too, made sure that there was always a positive in his songs, no matter how sad the subject matter.

And so the two had known one another for years when Jeff became involved with the album, as well as the single that was to be its calling card. "That song came in the middle of the process of putting together the album," he went on. "We were just having a jam session, tracking some things, and Bruno started playing this groove and making up something on the spot; we all thought it was pretty good. We wound up working a long time on that, trying to get it just right."

Of course, the rest of the Smeezingtons were as heavily involved as ever, and, increasingly sophisticated in the way they produced their sound, this time round they didn't even use instruments in some parts of the track. "On 'Locked Out Of Heaven' Bruno was like 'we need a dep-dep-dep-dep' sound,'" Ari told one interviewer. "I said, 'Sing it into the microphone' and then I chopped it up. It sounds like it's an instrument, but it's really his voice. We do that a lot."

As for Bruno himself, while he acknowledged the fact that it sounded a little like the Police, that had never been his actual intention. "Hell yeah! You try to write a Police song!" Bruno

Bruno shows off his drumming skills at KOKO in London, March 13, 2011. SIMONE JOYNER/GETTY IMAGES

Slave to the rhythm: Bruno at the 54th Annual Grammy Awards in Los Angeles, February 12, 2012. MARIO ANZUONI/REUTERS/CORBIS

The Mug shot of Bruno taken at the Clark County Detention Center in Las Vegas, September 19, 2010. AP PHOTO/LAS VEGAS METRO POLICE DEPARTMENT

Bruno consults with defense attorney Blair Berk during an appearance in court following the cocaine possession charge in Las Vegas. AP PHOTO/JULIE JACOBSON

Leather clad Bruno performs at the BBC Radio 1 Big Weekend at Ebrington Square in Londonderry, Northern Ireland, May 2013.

Latino beat: Bruno on stage at the Coliseo de Puerto Rico in San Juan, Puerto Rico, September 1, 2013.
PHOTOPRESS PR/SPLASH NEWS/CORBIS

Ziggy Marley, Bruno and Rihanna perform at the 55th Annual Grammy Awards at the Staples Center, Los Angeles, February 10, 2013.
KEVORK DJANSEZIAN/GETTY IMAGES

B.o.B. and Bruno Mars at Power 106 FMs Powerhouse at the Honda Centre, Anaheim, California, June 19, 2010.
STARTRAKS PHOTO/REX

Model Lily Aldridge and Bruno onstage during the 2012 Victoria's Secret Fashion Show at the Lexington Avenue Armory, New York, November 7, 2012. ENEWSIMAGE.COM/SPLASH NEWS

Flying high: Bruno and girlfriend Jessica Caban depart LMM International Airport in San Juan for their flight to Los Angeles, September 4, 2013. PHOTOPRESS PR/SPLASH NEWS/CORBIS

Bruno at Manchester Academy, March 10, 2011.

Left: Bruno and his father Peter Hernandez attend the 2013 MTV Video Music Awards at the Barclays Center in New York City, August 25, 2013, and, right, with his awards after the event. KEVIN MAZUR/WIREIMAGE FOR MTV , HENRY LAMB/PHOTOWIRE/BEI/REX

Bruno embraces Anthony Kiedis of Red Hot Chili Peppers during the halftime show of Super Bowl XLVIII at the MetLife Stadium in East Rutherford, New Jersey, February 2, 2014. PAUL BUCK/EPA/CORBIS

Bruno performs during the halftime show of the NFL Super Bowl football game between the Denver Broncos and the Seattle Seahawks in East Rutherford, New Jersey, February 2, 2014. CARLO ALLEGRI/REUTERS/CORBIS

told Yahoo Music. "I grew up listening to the Police, I grew up performing in bars, singing Police songs... I remember performing a song like 'Roxanne', and you play those first couple of chords, and you hit that first note, and you watch the whole bar ignite. And as an artist, as a songwriter, it's like 'Man, I want to write a song that makes people's eyes explode the first chord!' I don't think it initially tried to sound like anybody else, but I picked up the guitar and just started playing [the song's opening chords]. That's how it normally works; I'll pick up a guitar and I'll start humming a melody, and I started singing that, and I was up there in Sting-ville, in that register, so that's what you get..." Indeed, he and Sting went on to perform the song together at the 2013 Grammys.

If Bruno had been worried about whether his career was to be a flash in the pan, then this put him out of his misery. It was a global smash, becoming his fourth number one on the *Billboard* charts, topping Rihanna's 'Diamonds' in the process and breaking more records, in that Bruno got four number ones in a shorter space of time than any other solo male artist in 48 years since Bobby Vinton in a run that started in 1962. Bruno's place in the popular musical pantheon was assured.

The new album was in many ways to be very different from what had gone before, but Bruno was developing some trademark effects in his work and one of these was to be found in the video accompanying the single. Directed by Cameron Duddy and Bruno himself, who liked to have a hands-on aspect in every area of his work, the short film showed Bruno hanging out with his friends, smoking, drinking and loafing around, alongside being pictured with his band singing the song at a club. And, not for the first time, there was a very vintage feel to the whole thing, harping back to the era of VHS tapes; Bruno, although still only in his twenties, indulging in a very nostalgic note.

"The concept is just old-fashioned fun," Bruno told MTV

News. "No storyline, it's not me singing to a girl, you get a good sense of what you're going to get live... It's very VHS-y. I love that man, it takes me back to my childhood, when the tracking is off and the color is off, there's a beauty in that. You'd have to stand by the TV with, like, aluminium foil all over you."

Hugh McIntire of *Billboard* loved it. "Everything about 'Locked Out Of Heaven' -- whether it be the video or the track itself – is retro," he wrote. "While the song references the early discography of the Police, the video takes us back a little bit further. From the style of their dress and the wonky-TV effects on the video, one might guess that Bruno and his friends are partying in the seventies. Only the Akai MPC sampler being played by a band member reminds the viewer that this video is, in fact, modern." In fact, everyone else loved it as well, with the video winning Best Male Video during the 2013 MTV Video Music Awards.

On the whole, the critical reception of the song was excellent. Bill Lamb of About.com liked "Bruno Mars' sweet, gliding vocals", "strong relationship-centred lyrics" and "unique uptempo arrangement. It is pleasing to hear a strong mainstream pop song so uptempo without relying on ubiquitous dance club beats. This is a solid return for Bruno Mars." Jody Rosen of *Rolling Stone* said: "The song is about unbridled passion, but as usual with Mars, the aesthetic is tidy and impeccable, pop songcraft polished to a high-gloss gleam: jittery Police-esque rock-reggae verses that erupt, amid thunder-boom synths, into a steamrolling four-on-the-floor chorus." Andrew Unterberger of Popdust said the song was "raunchy yet subtle" and "classy enough not to get graphic or vulgar". He felt it was "hyper-energetic, funky, [and] slightly retro" but the "tiniest bit disappointing" that more was not added to the song's chorus. However, he said it was one of "the most fun, dynamic, and exciting songs" of 2012.

The good reviews went on. Carl Williott of Idolator praised it, saying it "shows an interesting musical evolution", and was "interesting". Neon Limelight said it was "irresistible" and "funky". Ryan Reed of *Paste Magazine* said it was "a driving pop anthem that moves from a punchy, 'Roxanne'-esque new-wave groove to a soulful, synth-driven chorus." Matt Cibula of PopMatters saw the Police influence: "It starts out like an early Police single, with some straight-up *Reggatta de Blanc* syncopation and a shockingly good Sting vocal impression. But the chorus opens up to turn into something less Police-y and more, dare I say it, Bruno Mars-y." He most certainly could dare to say it. Bruno was now an established musical presence, influential in his own right and creating art that, no matter what influences it absorbed from elsewhere, was recognisably all Bruno's own.

And on it went. Kitty Empire of *The Observer* said it "channels the Police, but its 21st-century builds owe as much to rave-pop as they do to producer Mark Ronson. It's an ill-omened meeting that somehow gels." Jason Lipshut of *Billboard* liked the single as much as his colleague had liked the video: "'Locked Out Of Heaven' is Mars' best solo single to date, with the singer-songwriter yelping about fornication as a tossed salad of chopped guitars and vocal exclamations buttress his sumptuous leading-man act," he wrote. "Sometimes, the perfect lead single is hard to find; other times, it walks right up to you and delivers a big, cozy hug."

Melinda Newman of HitFix liked "Mars' singing and the catchy little background vocals", which "keep the song moving downstream at a rapid pace. Even clumsy lyrics like 'your sex takes me to paradise' can't diminish that joy that the beats and melody bring." (Bruno was heard to remark on one radio show that that line actually referred to Halle Berry.) It was heady stuff and all went to prove one thing – Bruno was here to stay. In the meantime he continued to fit in promotional appearances, including the annual Victoria's Secret fashion show, where he performed alongside Rihanna and Justin Bieber, just the latest in a number of A-list stars who had adorned that particular catwalk. It was a gig from paradise for a bloke like Bruno with an eye for the girls, but his womanising days were over. He was now firmly with Jessica. Then there were more appearances on the British *X Factor*, which was all good publicity. In the wake of his appearance, sales of the single jumped by 67 per cent. Then there was a performance on *The Graham Norton Show*. Sales continued to soar.

The pace was pretty relentless, but then Bruno wanted it to be like this. Now that he'd got to the top, he wanted to stay there, and that involved working very hard. Success once tasted is not only sweet – it creates a need for it to be sustained and amongst everything else Bruno had to worry about, there was now the niggle that if he didn't work hard, it could all go away once more. Asked by the *Daily Mirror* if he was a workaholic, he replied, "I think so. I don't know how that happened, but I'm constantly moving. For this blood to run in my veins I need to be constantly doing something. It never stops. If I go watch a movie, I'm still thinking about chord progressions and stuff. I'm competitive with myself. I know when it's wrong and when it's right. And if there's something wrong with it I can't stop thinking about it." That also betrayed a perfectionist streak – and so much for the laid-back Hawaiian. The competitive spirit of Los Angeles was clearly now flowing in his veins.

He wasn't just a workaholic perfectionist, though. By this stage in the game Bruno was also brimming with confidence, as well he might. Sometimes people took this to be arrogance (it wasn't) but the truth is that it was necessary for the stage act and the stage persona, as Bruno pointed out when asked about it by *The Observer*. "You don't want to watch a guy with confidence?" he demanded. "You want to watch some nervous schmuck on stage? Or you want to watch someone who enjoys what he does and has confidence? Look at Michael Jackson and Prince and Elvis. Those guys exude confidence and those are the guys I grew up watching. Jackie Wilson. All those guys that are dancing and basically showing off. You know, when Michael Jackson does the moonwalk he's showing off! When Prince or Hendrix do a guitar solo, it's confidence! I would hate to be at a show and some nervous wreck is sweating up there and doesn't feel he deserves to be there." That man was not Bruno, who was loving every minute of his life.

And so to the all-important release of the album itself. Now that Bruno had proved himself with his first album, the record company was prepared to give him considerably more leeway with this, his second, and he had taken advantage of that to put together something that was more personal and rather different from the first. He tried to explain it as best he could.

"It turned into this soulful, experimental, electronic, hard-to-explain thing," he told americansongwriter.com. "That's the reason behind the album title – before I got signed to my current label, executives would always tell me what I did was too all over the place – too unorthodox. They couldn't imagine what radio station would play my stuff. I was thinking about this in my head when I started this album – so I decided to go into the studio and do whatever I wanted." And now he had the power to do exactly that.

Something else that Bruno both wanted and got was to work with the crème de la crème of the music industry. He'd worked with the best pretty much from the start, but now he could not only pick and choose – that crème de la crème were hollering to work with him. The list of people who contributed to the album read pretty much like a who's who of the music industry: jazz iconoclast Esperanza Spalding, EDM hitmaker Diplo, Jeff Bhasker, of course, and Mark Ronson, who had previously contributed a great deal to Amy Winehouse's success.

Ronson was surprised when he got the call, but glad at what happened next. "I was travelling in Zanzibar on my honeymoon when I got this call: 'Do you want to meet Bruno Mars?,'" he told Americansongwriter.com. "I was only kind of familiar with his music. But we met up in London a month later, and the first thing he said was, 'I want to sound exactly the opposite of what a Mark Ronson collaboration with Bruno Mars is supposed to sound like.' That won me over – and then I found out what a phenomenal talent he is. This is the most progressive music I've worked on yet. It's going to open up the arteries and change the sound of music." That was quite a claim – only people of the calibre of the Beatles could lay claim to changing the face of popular music, but that was the way people in the music industry were talking about Bruno now.

And so they got to work and Bruno, for one, was delighted with the results. "It's hard to create sounds with live instrumentation that bump in the club, and Mark Ronson did it here," he told Americansongwriter.com. "Since *Back To Black*, I've always wanted to get into his head and see how he does it."

"So much of the record is played live, but still sounds like a hit record on the radio," said Jeff. "This is Bruno showing new dimensions as a songwriter and producer." He particularly liked 'Old & Crazy', a duet with Esperanza Spalding that he said was a "kooky, true-jazz classic, like 'Pennies From Heaven'. It sounds like a song you'd hear in a club in twenties Paris, even though we recorded it on a laptop; we even use old microphones to give it that feel. It started with an Emile beat, and then I added a Django Reinhardt sample that I screwed with in Ableton; then Esperanza came in and nailed her bass and vocal parts live, like an old pro."

Bruno had already worked with Diplo on 'Liquor Store Blues' on *Doo-Wops & Hooligans* and he appeared here on 'Money Make Her Smile' about a gold digger. "That's the wild card," said Bruno. "Diplo has all the sounds in his computer to make the club go wild. We actually wrote that to be a strip-club anthem. After a concert in Paris, we went to a strip club; the promoter got on the mic and said, 'We have a special guest, Bruno Mars!' – and then they played 'Just The Way You Are'. That's the worst song to hear in that environment, so I resolved to write a good one."

It was an evening he harked back to more than once. "To make things worse, this poor girl comes out to dance, and he [the DJ] plays 'Just The Way You Are', which I'm sure is probably the last song a dancer wants to dance to," he told the *Daily Mirror*. "I just looked at her on the stage and said, 'I'm sorry!' I was like, if that ever happens to me again, I wanna make sure I got the right song. So I wrote a song called 'Money Maker Smile'."

Everyone involved in the making of the new work was full of praise for the rising superstar. Diplo himself couldn't have spoken more highly of Bruno. "In our generation, he's the most talented guy I've worked with," he said. "That record, he wanted to have something for the club that has some noise on it and an 'I don't give a fuck' feel. Still, he writes giant pop songs. Bruno just does things with the songwriting I could never do – I've never spent so much time working on a bridge or post-chorus, but that's what you have to do." He told another journalist that the album was this generation's *Thriller*, and praise didn't come much higher than that. And he may well have been right: reviewing the album, *The Times* said, "The soul-informed 'If I Knew', which closes the album, proves Mars is a classicist at heart, and a potential inheritor of Michael Jackson's pop crown." The comparisons with Jackson in fact came from every quarter, again heralding much for the future ahead.

Not that he didn't have some detractors. The album was not to receive totally positive reviews and there were some naysayers who were not entirely fans, not least those who were saying that Bruno was still too close in style to some of the musicians he had once impersonated. Michael Jackson fans didn't appreciate being told that Bruno was heir to the great man and when comparisons were made, it was not always favourable to Bruno. His constant appearances in a fedora recalled Jackson in his heyday, too, which also didn't help. But Bruno was getting beyond worrying about criticism: he had so comprehensively proved himself that he clearly didn't care much what anyone else thought.

"Yeah, you know, people aren't going to love everything you do," he said in an interview with the *Independent On Sunday*. "And you gotta realise that that's the way the world is today, especially with the internet and Facebook and Twitter; everyone has an opinion. And it's gonna be more in your face because of the times we're living in, so the sooner you realise that, at the end of the day, no one's opinion matters, the sooner you're gonna have fun. And I'm having a fucking blast, sweetheart."

Not that he needed to worry. The reviews were by no means uniformly favourable, but enough people were giving it the thumbs up for Bruno to rest easy. Simon Gage in the UK's *Daily Express* liked it. "It's the genre-hopping that makes Mars so interesting with the music very much on the acoustic side, the voice avoiding the usual wittering of current R&B and good old-fashioned quality songs giving the package a timeless feel," he wrote.

Andy Gill in *The Independent* felt that Bruno was so influenced by other artists he was having to mirror their former glories, but he, too, was won round in the end. "But it's the closing dip into deep-soul pleading on 'If I Knew' that assures the brightness of his future: for once, it's just a style, not a specific copy of another artist, and it allows Bruno the space to express his own sweet character," he wrote.

Kitty Empire in *The Observer* also made the comparison with Jackson (although she did remark that he wasn't quite in the same league) and went on: "Listening to his second album, you can easily see why this capable, versatile man is so successful. In the fraught, loud, ADD world of pop production, Mars' songs value narrative arc and internal logic; his soundscapes have three dimensions. Every element isn't just yelling at you from the front."

Over in the States, reviews were also mixed. Jody Rosen of *Rolling Stone* said it was "the stuff of great pop" and "a record that makes the competition sound sad and idea-starved by comparison". Matt Cibula of PopMatters felt it was "sung and arranged just as perfectly as his earlier work... a truly accomplished and slick pop album". Melissa Maerz of *Entertainment Weekly* opined "his talent for crafting little pop perfections of all stripes is undeniable". Jon Caramanica of *The New York Times* said the songs were "exceptionally drawn and lush".

Dan Hyman of *Spin* felt it was "utterly engaging" and Bruno's lyrics "get a desperately needed kick in the pants". Jason Lipshutz of *Billboard* said it "succeeds in mixing its safer stylistic choices with its relatively bold ideas." Ryan Reed of *Paste* felt that Mars "still plays the sweetheart card well, but he's proven himself way more interesting as a badass".

Allmusic's Tim Sendra said that Bruno was an "icky hater" and his "opinion of the opposite sex seems to have taken a nosedive" after "being a sweet romancer" on his first album. *Slant Magazine* was cautious about Bruno's "variety-show mimicry" and viewed his "workmanlike" singing as both a "minor limitation" and "the key to his appeal", with the album being "a reasonably listenable exercise in genre fetishisation". Tony Clayton-Lea of *The Irish Times* said its songs "may be in serious hock to their sources, but Mars has a snappy way with rhythms and rhymes. No killer, then, but no filler, either." Touché.

Chapter 11

The Sacred And The Profane

By the end of 2012, Bruno and Jessica were now an established couple. Rumours of their impending engagement came and went, but Bruno was now openly talking about being ready to settle down and a future involving children and marriage. But the path of true love never runs entirely smooth, and it hadn't for those two, either. There was the odd bumpy patch, as there is in any relationship, and the odd row. And it was during one of these that Bruno seriously feared the relationship would come to an end – Jessica was, after all, a beautiful, sought-after woman – which in turn gave rise to one of his most successful songs to date.

'When I Was Your Man', the third single from *Unorthodox Jukebox*, was a massive, worldwide hit. A somewhat yearning ballad about the pre-fame days and the girl who got away – which somehow gave the incorrect impression that it was written about Rita Ora – Bruno sang sadly about how he hoped her new man was giving her the love that he, Bruno, could not.

Bruno had always used his personal experiences as the basis for his songs, but this one was far more personal than any had ever been before. Fans were first given a hint of this when he tweeted a photograph of the artwork for *Unorthodox Jukebox*: "Soon you guys will hear a song called 'When I Was Your Man'," he added. "I've never been this nervous. Can't explain it."

The song was written in conjunction with Andrew Wyatt (the Smeezingtons, as always, were also involved). Again and again Bruno emphasised the importance of the song to himself: "When we started the record I was like, 'I'm never singing another ballad again,' but that came from the gut – it's the most honest thing I've ever sung," he told *Rolling Stone*. "When there are no safe bets, that's when I feel my gut move." It was not clear whether "no safe bets" referred to the success or otherwise of the record's performance – or of the underlying relationship itself.

It wasn't just Bruno who felt strongly about the song. His fellow Smeezingtons seemed to have been similarly affected, even if they didn't have the emotional input that Bruno did. "I think Bruno and I are both huge fans of older music, like Billy Joel and Elton John. We always loved those moments where you can sit at the piano and emote," said Philip. "Those intimate moments when an artist is so naked and vulnerable; you can't help but be drawn to it. We always wanted to find a stripped down song like that, which is how that song came to be. The subject matter was real life; Bruno had experienced that, so we tried to say it in the best and catchiest way we could."

When it was released, it was an absolute smash hit, with the usual tumbling of records that Bruno could have been forgiven for starting to expect whenever a new release came out. The single became his tenth number to make it to the *Billboard* Top 10 and as it entered the magic circle, Bruno became the first man to have two titles as a lead act in the Hot 100's Top 10 ('Heaven' was still at number two) since, er, Bruno himself, who had managed a similar feat with 'Grenade' and 'Just The Way You Are'. Ultimately it got to number one, making it only the second song to do so in the chart's 50-odd year history to be exclusively piano and vocals (the other was Adele's 'Someone Like You') as well as soaring up the charts in various locations around the world.

The accompanying video was as melancholic in tone as the ballad warranted, although as so often, Bruno was channelling a seventies vibe in the short film. It showed him sitting at the piano, sunglasses on, a half-drunk glass of whisky at his side; the director was Cameron Duddy, with whom Bruno so frequently collaborated. It was as professional as everyone had come to expect, but the whole production, both video and song, had taken Bruno to another level. There was something raw about this, a real show of emotion from the charming, laid-back kid from Hawaii. To put it at its most basic, it showed that Bruno was not just a pretty boy singer. He had depth.

The critics, on the whole, were pretty impressed by it, as well. Sam Lanksy of Idolator said it was "an emotional ballad that shows off Mars' sweet vocals... another exceptional offering from *Unorthodox Jukebox*, which is shaping up to be one of the year's best pop releases." (Perhaps it really was going to be the current generation's *Thriller*.) Andrew Unterberger of Popdust said it was "a much more satisfying, less ostentatious ballad than 'Young Girls' – though maybe the lyrics are a little too clichéd to result in a classic soul ballad the way Bruno seems to be going for... [But] nobody puts a song like this over quite like him, and when he hits the big high note on the song's bridge, it's about as striking a moment as you're likely to hear on a pop record this year. It might be a little too perfect to be as devastating as a song like 'Someone Like You' but it might be a big hit just the same, and it's guaranteed to absolutely slay in a live set."

Melissa Maerz of *Entertainment Weekly* said "Old-school charm still gets Mars the furthest, and the best thing here is the classic torch song 'When I Was Your Man', which finds him at the piano listing all the ways he wronged an ex. 'Caused a good, strong woman like you to walk out my life,' he cries in his Sinatra-smooth tenor, oozing charm. Maybe he's a jerk. But he's the jerk that girl's going home with tonight." The Sinatra comparison was also apposite: no one could sing a torch song like Sinatra. Bruno was in pretty good company there.

Jon Caramanica of *The New York Times* felt that, "The piano tells it all on this song, which is one of the most certain on the album... If this isn't the beginning of the Billy Joel comeback, people should lose their jobs." Jason Lipshut of *Billboard* wrote "it will make for a killer lighters-in-the-air moment in concert. Although it's not quite an Alicia Keys-esque powerhouse, 'When I Was Your Man' smartly allows Mars to momentarily remove his fedora and bare his soul." Jessica Sager of Pop Crush felt, "It's a vulnerable look at the ever-smooth Mars, and if it doesn't pull at your heartstrings at least a little bit, you might not have a soul." Jim Farber of *New York Daily News* wrote that, "He matches his bravura performance to a tune stirring enough to inspire aspiring stars on the *X Factor/Idol* axis for years to come."

Melinda Newman of HitFix said it was a "beautiful piano ballad... There's not a lot of embellishment, there are no samples and there is not a wasted note." Sandy Cohen of *The Huffington Post* wrote: "Mars is at his best on the bare piano ballad 'When I Was Your Man'." Andrew Chan of *Slant Magazine*, however, was not so complimentary. He felt that "his melody and lyrics end up sounding as slight as they did before – an embarrassment for an artist who's staked so much of his image on sturdy, old-fashioned songcraft." But that was not the consensus among the critics and certainly not among the fans, who were buying the record in their droves.

It was difficult to do what Bruno had done – to admit that this song was deeply personal to him, that it touched on feelings he had really had and that it showed him to be vulnerable, after all. His public persona was after all very much a cheeky chappy, sometimes bordering on the arrogant, who took life in a happy-go-lucky way, enjoying the success that was his and up for a good time. This song showed him in a very different light: as someone who could be and had been hurt. But to reveal this to the world took guts – it was one thing to sing about how much he wanted to be a billionaire and something quite different to expose a corner of his heart. He was aware of this himself.

"I feel silly talking about my insecurities, kinda embarrassed," he told *The Examiner*. The song started out with a few simple chords, reflecting on regrets... "Like I shoulda brought you flowers. It's tough talking about this song and performing it is even more difficult. Yes it has a happy ending in reality but I can't imagine the song turning into reality."

Matters with Jessica were clearly going well. And it was a rare emotional display that he didn't often allow himself – "I'm not a fan of self-indulgence, music is for me to feel good and to dance," was how he put it. "Ain't nobody wanna hear me sing about growing up in Hawaii and give them a sob story. It's all about positive, baby." And unknown to many, there was a sob story or two to be had about the Hawaiian childhood – the bullying, the parental divorce and the difficult stage in his father's business. But Bruno didn't talk about any of this very much.

Nevertheless, he was prepared to be very open about the song. In an interview in *On Air With Ryan Seacrest*, he was more forthcoming still. "Everything that I write is from a genuine honest place because at the end of the day I have to connect with the song," he said. "And I have to perform the song. I can't just be singing fairytales and putting on an act basically – talk about something that is extremely hard to talk about and be as honest as possible. So you know, I'm in a situation right now, when you write that song you're in a dark studio and bringing out those emotions and tapping into a dark place... and now I'm at a part where I'm performing it... and it's a very eerie, weird feeling because you're like bleeding in front of people talking about this personal thing that happened to you. So I'm going through that right now… I've never felt anything like it before. You can't really hide from it. If you don't treat her good, someone else will."

But, as much as the song clearly meant a great deal to him, life had to go on, and with it the relentless schedule of touring, entertaining and preparing new music. Bruno really had become part of the cultural fabric now – he was very amused when he discovered that men had started using his track 'Marry Me' to propose to their loved ones – and was continuing to garner huge amounts of attention. Appearing at the Grammys in February 2013, where he was nominated for an award as producer and writer of 'Young, Wild And Free' – sung by Snoop Dogg and Wiz Khalifa and featuring Bruno – although he ultimately lost out to Niggas in Paris. Even so, the evening was a good showcase for Bruno: as well as singing with Sting, he also performed with Rihanna, Ziggy Marley and Damian Marley in a tribute to Bob Marley.

By this time Bruno was becoming known for his love songs and so it was no surprise when the next single, 'Treasure' (his woman is his treasure), turned out to be just that. Whereas his previous hit was a soulful ballad, however, this one ran an unashamed disco vibe: another Smeezingtons production, it was based on the idea that boys just wanted to have fun. "Well, the thing we learned after touring with *Doo-Wops* was how it is we like to feel on stage when performing. We're fun, like to dance and party, and we didn't really get to do a lot of that on the first album," Philip Lawrence told *American Songwriter*. "It's the kind of song where the whole band can get up and jam and have this Earth, Wind And Fire kind of moment."

Although it didn't do quite as well as its predecessor, 'Treasure' was another global success. Again the accompanying video channelled the seventies, referencing Earth, Wind And Fire's 'Let's Groove'; it also featured a dancer, although this time it was Taja Riley, rather than Jessica. The critics loved it: Michael Lopez from *The Huffington Post* said, "Flossing a bright red blazer and a hefty afro, the part-Puerto Rican crooner looks like he time travelled to a vintage Euro discotheque. But to be honest, the trend works! And it's certainly helped by 'Treasure''s bouncy beats." Kyle Anderson from *EW* remarked that, "We should probably just change the name of this year from 2013 to 1978, because there are more sparkly suits and disco guitars than we know what to do with... Bruno Mars has gone full-on Betamax for his new video for the track 'Treasure'. It's all there: the suits, the setting, and the bong–water video effects." They were not alone in their approval: along with everything else, Bruno choreographed the whole thing (that childhood experience as a dancer continued to be an enormous boon) and was rewarded for his efforts at the 2013 MTV Video Music Awards when he won an award for Best Choreography. He also won an award at the ceremony for Best Male Video for 'When I Was Your Man', marking him out as one of the most versatile stars of the day.

The song itself got a good reception, too. In truth, Bruno could probably sing the 'Alphabet Song' these days and still have a hit on his hands, but it was still important that the critics liked what he did and so it proved. Jason Lipshutz of *Billboard* said one "gets the feeling that 'Treasure', with its grand harmonies, classically kooky hooks and slyly sexual undertones, is the musical mode that makes Mars the happiest". He was right there – with his love of seventies disco, you could almost say that Bruno had been born 40 years too late. Melissa Maerz of *Entertainment Weekly* said the song "makes silk–jumpsuit disco feel contemporary", and Caroline Sullivan of *The Guardian* described the song as a "sprightly disco thumper".

Robert Copsey of Digital Spy said that Bruno "insists over eighties smooth funk guitars and retro-styled disco beats, before declaring his woman his 'treasure' and 'golden star' with a sense of unabashed affection. The result sounds like a modern day 'Rock With You'; a feat that few could get away with pulling off so authentically." *Rolling Stone*'s Jody Rosen found it "a creamy Michael Jackson/Prince-schooled disco soul" and Matt Cibula from Pop Matters said it "knows that a flirt beats a bleat any day". Matthew Horton from BBC Music described it as "sugary early eighties funk", and said that it "is lathered in so much slap bass it starts to sting". Ryan Reed of Paste Magazine said, "'Treasure' is stripper-theme funk-pop with gooey synth pads and enormous slap-bass fills that punch through like air-humps." All were pretty much in agreement, however – Bruno had produced another great track.

He was about to produce another, too, although this one was going to be considerably more controversial than anything he had done before. 'Gorilla' was another love song, of sorts, but this time round it was a paean to wild, animal sex. It raised quite a few eyebrows (some of Bruno's fans were on the young side) and lyrics like "I got a body full of liquor/With a cocaine kicker" were felt to be pretty close to the bone, given Bruno's recent travails. But Bruno didn't want to appeal just to a very young fanbase: he wanted to be an adult star, addressing adult issues, and so he was prepared to take the risk.

Bruno himself was confident about it – as indeed he was about all his work. "I felt 'Young Girls' was good," he told MTV. "'Locked Out Of Heaven' was something brand new I tried in the studio and it felt like the right thing to do. None of these things are planned, which one goes first, which one goes second. One day I wake up and I say, 'You know what? I want the world to hear this song that I wrote called 'Young Girls', and I put it out." And so to the latest track, and how he intended to handle that. "Every day I'm thinking about the video," he continued. "It's going to be something I've never done before, I promise you that. On the album *Unorthodox Jukebox* there's a gorilla on the album cover because I wrote a song called 'Gorilla'. And that was the first song we wrote for this album and it really set the tone for the entire project and it kind of became the mascot. Why not put it on the cover?" Why not indeed?

Bruno had been singing the song on tour, but it reached a wider audience when he performed it on the 2013 MTV Video Music Awards. The critics loved it. "There's something to be said about simplicity when whatever's simply being done is awesome," said *Billboard*'s Brad Wete. "Bruno Mars never moved more than three steps in any direction during his performance of new single 'Gorilla'. But boy, did he sing! His voice soared and his passion was palpable as he performed the bedroom jam. Sure, it'd be tough to find many people who watched the VMAs for Bruno specifically. Names like Timberlake and Gaga eclipse his celebrity. But when his time came, Mars left his mark."

Mathew Jacobs of *The Huffington Post* also thought that the performance was quite exceptional. "Mars was accompanied by a horn section, and the jazzy new song marked one of the night's tamer moments, even as blasts of fire erupted during the chorus. Amid an evening filled with sensual performances, Mars offered a brand of artistry unmatched by the bulk of the telecast."

Entertainment Weekly also felt it was the highlight of the evening, calling it, "The most elegantly designed and executed performance of the evening... Mars, who performed 'Gorilla', standing behind a mic stand high up on a simple platform, with a giant gorilla face behind him, lasers shooting through the room, and his crack band booting the whole thing along. But although there was a unified feel, with Mars staying put and the colour scheme a consistent glowing green, there was plenty of drama – three parts human, with Mars belting with tremendous feeling and kicking over his mic stand, and one part fire, with the night's biggest pyrotechnics shooting off at the climax."

Bruno's fellow celebrities had taken note of what was going on on stage and were keen to show their admiration too. Skylar Grey tweeted: "Best voice, no one does it like Bruno Mars", Ed Sheeran described the performance as "the best performance of the night", Pharrell Williams congratulated Mars for his win while Hilary Duff called 'Gorilla' "straight baby making music". But not everyone was happy. In Britain, GIRLS education campaigner Dannielle Miller told the *Daily Telegraph*: "As a mum of young kids I get offended when I hear lyrics where men refer to women as sluts. This is not a song that respects women. Anyone who asks you to call them 'daddy' in the bedroom is just 50 shades of wrong. How would you [Bruno] feel about someone saying that to your daughter?" In actual fact, although the song was far raunchier than his usual fare, it had to be said that Bruno was usually far more respectful of women than many of his fellow pop stars. But here, it seemed, he wanted to have a bit of fun.

And so to the making of the video. Bruno called in his old friend Cameron Duddy: the idea was to film it in a strip club, but because they couldn't find the right venue, they built one all for themselves. At least it made for some enjoyable research: "Me and Bruno went to probably seven or eight strip clubs, you know, for research," Cameron told MTV. "We'd be in there on, say, a Tuesday night, we'd walk in, and the few people that were actually in there were watching the dancers, but we'd be looking at the architecture of the place for inspiration. And then we'd have our one drink and leave."

It was a pretty hands-on effort, with the men creating something that looked as if it could have come out of Havana. They even painted the walls themselves – Bruno's obsessive attention to detail had clearly not gone away. "I don't know when Bruno sleeps, if he does at all," Cameron continued. "He's the hardest-working person I've ever worked with or met. He pays attention to everything; he's the one who came up with the basic idea for this video, when he was rehearsing for his tour in, like, Cleveland. We'd have conversations about it, then later, he'd call me at 2 a.m. and be like 'We gotta do this' or 'We need to add that.'"

In another move that raised eyebrows, the actress Freida Pinto appeared in the video playing a stripper and indeed, she really did strip. "I've got to tip my hat to Bruno for that one," said Cameron. "We wanted to do a stripper, and we wanted a name, but there were no other names thrown around besides Freida Pinto. And I said 'Aw man, she's so safe, it may be difficult if you go that route.' And he was like 'Listen dude, it's important to the video to use someone who hasn't been seen in this light before.' It was a gamble, and I wasn't all the way sure about it, but I trusted his instincts... and he was right. She's an actress, so for her, it was about grasping her character's background, and then getting up there and doing it."

The video was certainly somewhat saucier than Bruno's usual fare and at six minutes in length was venturing towards short film territory (more parallels with Michael Jackson). It opened with a pair of arguing strippers fixing their make-up backstage, sniping about a new stripper called Isabella (Freida) fooling around with Bruno, with the women saying, "Wait till I tell the boss who she's been sleeping with." It emerges that Frieda has heard everything: she goes on stage and starts pole dancing, before disrobing amidst a shower of sparks. Scenes follow of Frieda and Bruno in the back seat of a car cut with scenes of her with customers, until at the end Bruno turns into a giant gorilla. Subtle it was not.

But who cares about subtle when you've made an impact? The critics loved it: James Montgomery from MTV said: "His latest clip is undoubtedly indebted to the past few decades of pop-cultural history... yet, once again, he's managed to created something entirely new, too... Thanks to Pinto's wattage, 'Gorilla' goes to heights – and depths – Mars has never visited before... Bruno pushes practically everything to the max... we're all riding along with him, and we can't wait to go back, even if we probably need to take a cold shower before repeated viewings." Even after reading the review, let alone watching the video, the fans were out of breath.

Ray Rahman from *Entertainment Weekly* said it "is set in a seedy tequila-soaked strip joint and features *Slumdog Millionaire* actress Frieda Pinto getting in down-and-dirty mode; she pole dances, licks guitars, and gets skintimate with Mars in the back of a car." Idolator's Carl Williott said that "the stylish visual, which was directed by Mars and Cameron Duddy, maintains the sweaty nightclub vibe established in the 'Locked Out Of Heaven' video. There's a loose narrative centred around Pinto's character Isabella, a new dancer to whom Mars has taken a liking, much to the chagrin of the club's veteran strippers."

And so what of the actual song? Bruno was well outside his comfort zone (though enjoying every minute of it) but according to some of the critics, at least, his gamble had paid off. Jason Lipshutz of *Billboard* said it was "an ambitious arena-rock sex jam that cannot overcome its main lyric: 'You and me, baby, making love like gorillas!' The drums and keyboards are nicely overwhelming, but the overall concept floats too far away to make a dent on the listener." *Spin*'s Dan Hyman commented that Bruno "scatters a slew of f-bombs throughout, most notably on the Prince-channelling, Diplo-produced hump-fest 'Gorilla', wherein he woos a seemingly willing lover ('Give it to me, mothafucka') after laying bare his own failings ('I got a body full of liquor and a cocaine kicker'), not referencing his Vegas bathroom-stall drug arrest back in September 2010." A low blow, that.

Sputnikmusic's disappearhere was not so keen: " 'Gorilla' is a slow paced 80s like ballad that has distorted power chords, electronic drums, and a driving vocal line, however despite this, the track is probably another low point, which occurring this early in the album makes me not like the album's structure and song order that much. The lyrics of this song also don't do much for me, I mean seriously 'You'll be banging on my chest, Bang bang, gorilla, You and me baby making love like gorillas' isn't the most deeply written or meaningful thing I've ever heard."

In *The Washington Post*, Allison Stewart was also not totally sold. "The formerly mild-to-the-point-of-possibly-being-dead Mars maps out a night of romance. It begins with "a body full of liquor with a cocaine kicker" and ends with "you and me/ Making love like gorillas." Anyone who has spent any amount of time watching *Animal Planet* would not find this much of an inducement, but hear him out: 'Gorilla', for all its awfulness, is just the sort of image-shifter Mars needs."

"It's the follow-up to 'Our First Time' from his previous album, which delves into (you guessed it) the first time he got intimate with a particular girl. And yet again, the libidinous lyrics are disguised with epic guitars and Phil Collins-esque heavy drum combinations that could make it strong enough to soundtrack a scene in a drama series," said Emily Tan from Idolator.

It must be said, women were much more down on the track than men. Amy Dawson of *Metro* said it was a "Phil Collins-esque low point" in the album "in which the button-eyed singer makes plans to go at it in the same way as said giant ape, all over a Phil Collins-esque synth/percussion combo backing... but by the time the jungle noises kick in, you think he surely must be in on the joke."

Nor were the public totally sold on the idea: the single performed markedly less well than some of Bruno's others. But he had made his point: he wasn't just a pretty boy, baby-faced singer always crooning about the sweeter side of love. This Bruno was all man.

Chapter 12

Tragedy Strikes

Bruno was on top of the world. Things could not possibly have been better: 'Gorilla' might have attracted a little controversy, but there was no publicity that was bad publicity. Bruno had achieved more than he could possibly have dreamed of. In a couple of years he had gone from total unknown to global superstar. And he was enjoying the controversy: "Let's just say I'm in beast mode now," he told *The Sun*. "I've shown that lover-boy side of me – does anyone really want me to come back and sing 'Just The Way You Are Part Two'? As much as I love that song, I feel like I need to express other areas of love, relationships, girls and sex." Or to put it another way, Bruno wanted to show that he was not a boy, but a man.

But he was not above asking people who'd been in the business a while for advice. Bruno was loving his success so much that he certainly didn't want it to slip away, but he was very aware that, difficult as it was to make it in the entertainment industry, it was even harder to stay at the top. It was a precarious life, as he'd discovered with the cocaine incident, when he'd risked losing everything, and to keep going was not always as easy as it looked.

And so he turned to someone who really knew what it took to maintain a career in the music industry – Lionel Richie.

The singer, who had had massive hits with 'Hello' and 'Three Times A Lady', was surprised and delighted to be asked for advice. "The new generation are discovering that guys like me can do melodies," he told the *Daily Star*. "Bruno Mars is a killer for melodies and lyrics, and he came to my show. He asked me afterwards 'Can you tell me how you do it?' and I said: 'Don't worry, you're doing just fine.' These new guys are hungry for longevity. Daft Punk's album shares some of that R&B sound, and they know it's all about writing great songs." And no one could write songs better than Bruno.

Touring continued (including gigs with Rita Ora) and Bruno closed the show at BBC Radio 1's Big Weekend, a very prestigious slot which marked quite how far he had come. His popularity continued to rise. But, of course, life has a habit of causing unpleasantness when it was least expected and so it was to prove. In May 2013, Bruno was alerted to the fact that his mother, Bernadette, had collapsed at home in Honolulu with a heart attack and been rushed to Queens Medical Centre in Honolulu. He returned to the Hawaiian capital immediately, but it was too late. Bernadette, who had remarried to Kip Botelho, died of a brain aneurism at the age of just 55. Bruno and his siblings were shattered: they had all been very close and Bruno had frequently credited his mother with instilling in him a love of music. He even had a tattoo on his arm bearing the legend "Bernadette". His first ever song, aged four, had been called 'I Love You Ma'. And now this.

It was little comfort that Bernadette had seen her son make such a spectacular success of his life, however: the family was knocked for six. Bruno's sisters Jaime and Presley both took to Twitter to express their grief ("The most beautiful girl in the world," tweeted Presley, who attached a picture of the young

Bernadette performing hula. "Until forever. I love you Ma.")
Condolences poured in to Bruno and the family, from the fans as
well as celebrities such as Rihanna and Randy Jackson. "Sending
my love and condolences to @BrunoMars at this difficult time!
I'm sincerely praying for you bro! #1Love" Rihanna tweeted.

"Terrible news. Praying for you @brunomars" tweeted Randy
Jackson.

Jennifer Love Hewitt said: "My heart is breaking for Bruno
Mars and his family tonight. I know all too well, too recent and
too deep what they are feeling. my prayers."

The local newspaper, the *Honolulu Pulse*, ran an obituary:
"Bernadette Bayot may have been better known the world over
as the mother of Bruno Mars, but family and friends in Hawaii
remember her as a beloved and respected member of the local
entertainment community."

It also quoted the performer Tommy D, who knew the family.
"It should be noted that Bernie was a very talented lady herself
and a good mother to Bruno," he said. "With Bruno she was a
mother to him first, always reminding him to do his chores and
help clean up the dressing room." (Bruno, then 16, was doing a
Michael Jackson act.) "Bernie was the triple threat, an all-around
entertainer, producer and choreographer."

Bruno was looking shell-shocked throughout, although after
a few days he too was able to take to Twitter, not least to thank
his fans for all their messages of support: "So thankful for all the
love during the most difficult time in my life. Ill [sic] be back on
my feet again soon. Thats [sic] what mom wants, she told me,"
he wrote.

But everything was different now. All through the years of
struggle, Bruno had at least had the rock-solid support of his
family behind him and he had also had their pride in what he
had achieved. So much of his identity, and his musical roots, was
bound up in his family, that for Bruno, the change was quite

difficult to comprehend. And Bernadette had been so young – only 55. There had been no lengthy illness, no warnings that her life was about to be cut short, no time to prepare himself, and the shock to everyone was enormous. Bruno might have been an adult, but to lose a parent at any stage is a terrible wrench and so it was to prove with him.

Grief-stricken as he was, Bruno had to get back to work. He was just embarking on the Moonshine Jungle tour, in support of *Unorthodox Jukebox* and so, after a period of mourning, it was back on the road again. In many ways this was a good thing: at least Bruno had a distraction, something to try to take his mind off what had happened. But it was still a terrible blow and it could not have been helped by the fact that there was some public speculation on Bruno forums about whether the tour would go ahead. No one wanted to be tactless, but it was a little unfortunate that bereavement got caught up with whether Bruno's fans would be disappointed. In the event they were not.

It was a sign of his professionalism that just a few weeks later Bruno was in Washington DC to start the tour: his set list was as follows: 'Natalie', 'Treasure', 'Money It's What I Want', 'Billionaire', 'Show Me', 'Candy Rain', 'Our First Time', 'Pony', 'Marry You', 'If I Knew', 'Runaway Baby', 'Young Girls', 'When I Was Your Man', 'Grenade', 'Just the Way You Are', 'Locked Out Of Heaven' and 'Gorilla', a testament to how far he'd come over the last couple of years and what a major star he now was. Hit after hit was familiar to the crowd – and yet they had all just been produced in the previous few years. Here was the man who was so often dubbed the new Michael Jackson showing off an impressive back catalogue that had not even existed just a couple of years previously. Nor was Bruno going to make public his private grief. He was a major star now and was preparing to give it all he had.

The tour was different from the last one. That had taken place mainly in theatres and ballrooms, but now, given that Bruno's star had risen so sharply, it was to take place in arenas – risky, because although it mirrored Bruno's new status, it also meant there was a danger of empty seats. In the event, however, most of the shows had sold out. Before the news about his mother, Bruno had been preparing himself for this much more onerous tour: "He spends a lot of time rehearsing and preparing, and directing and doing choreography, everything," Bruno's manager, Brandon Creed, told *Billboard* in an interview that spring. "It's all him... He takes it from the past and brings it to today. Wait till you see the tour. We're going into rehearsals now, so I don't have much to share, but it's going to be... incredible. It's hectic, but it's amazing... It's a thrill to work with an artist so talented."

A lot was at stake, but Bruno was to show himself more than capable of rising to the challenge. And it was to be a lengthy undertaking. It kicked off in the States in June 2013, moved to Europe in the autumn and finished in New Zealand and Australia in the spring of 2014. Opening acts were lined up: Fitz and the Tantrums followed by Ellie Golding for the first leg of the tour, Mayer Hawthorne for Europe and Miguel for the Antipodes. Again, it had not been so long since Bruno was a backing act. Everything had changed.

Bruno was really going for it, though, pulling at all the stops to create a spectacular that fans and critics alike would enjoy. And indeed, the critics raved. "Sprawling video screens. Blasts of smoke, fire and confetti. A disco ball the size of a Toyota Prius," wrote Chris Richards in *The Washington Post*, on the fact that Bruno was yet again re-creating his beloved seventies/eighties era, just as he had done in so many of his videos. "The performance of the singer who sold out Washington's Verizon Center was one of those rare, thrilling, upside-down pop concerts where instead of rigidly trying to re-create the high sheen of various hit singles, the singer takes complete control of the songbook, reshaping it at will. Which is to say, it was fantastic... [He] hopscotched through Motown, new wave, late-seventies funk, mid–nineties R&B, flaunting a pop fluency that's earned him a vast and diverse horde of admirers. You could see it in Saturday night's audience – there were baby boomers, babies of boomers, babies of babies of boomers, and in Section 100, an actual baby. [But] Put the Hooligans, the name of the backing band, on that ticket stub, too." It would scarcely have been possible to get a more positive review than that and while it certainly didn't make up for his recent bereavement, it did, at least, give Bruno something to smile about again.

Sarah Rodman of *The Boston Globe* was another fan: "14,785 fans in attendance left with more than a few beads of perspiration on their brows thanks to the indefatigable singer-songwriter's ecstatic approach to performing... The energy never flagged as Mars displayed his flair for dramatics and classic showmanship, twisting, thrusting, and shimmying through retro soul jams... Mars has chosen his band wisely as they not only bring his music to life but match his enthusiasm and hit every step alongside the boss... Clearly, much work, planning, and rehearsal went in to the show, but Mars made it look easy."

Everyone else was pretty ecstatic as well. Jason Lipshutz of *Billboard*, who had been charting and commenting on Bruno's career from the start, was one of the many people to notice that he could turn his hand to just about anything. His review reflected that. "Mars' biggest asset as a performer has always been his ambidextrousness, and in his current stage show, the singer holds high notes, leads choreographed dances, plays electric guitar, plays acoustic guitar, plays drums, engages the crowd and even flirts with some ladies in the front row," he wrote. "He's a convincing 'whole package' kind of pop artist, and like an ace Pixar movie with 'in' jokes for parents, he expertly caters to his older and younger demographics at his live shows... His pop tracks may not possess enriching messages, but his tirelessness and dedication must be appreciated when seen in person. And appreciate it they did: when all was said and done, the Wells Fargo Center in Philadelphia roared with a collective dizziness usually reserved for the all-too-occasional Flyers playoff win."

And everyone loved Bruno's immersion in the glory days of disco. Jim Farber of *New York Daily News* said the "show aimed to re-create a bygone era of flashy entertainment, a disco-age, tip-of-the-fedora to natty, seventies acts like the Jacksons, the Tramps and the Bee Gees... Befitting his Pacific rearing, Mars' music has an island ease and warmth... It hardly seemed to matter that the show wasn't big on risk or depth."

This was all the more remarkable given that Bruno was still reeling from the loss of his mother, but his innate professionalism meant that he was not allowing himself to share his inner pain. Indeed, life had to go on: he teamed up with his old friend Diplo to work on a song called 'Bubble Butt', which also featured the US rapper 2 Chainz. "Bruno and me were working on tracks for the No Doubt record, so we did this for fun," he told *The Sun*. "I know (indie blog) Pitchfork said 'Bubble Butt' is the worst song of the year but, for me, it's the biggest record we've ever done. Credibility doesn't matter to me at all. I've never had credibility - I'm a white dude doing reggae!"

And they weren't the only people who wanted to work with Bruno. Katy Perry became the latest to put her name on the list: "I have always said I would wanna collaborate with Rihanna but I'd love to collaborate with Bruno Mars," she told the *Daily Mirror*. "I always say, 'When I grow up, I wanna be the female version of Bruno Mars', cause he's so wildly talented in showing everybody that he has so much diversity in him." But these days, just about everyone wanted a piece of Bruno.

The tour moved to Europe and it was the turn of the European critics to pass judgement. Malcolm Jack in *The Guardian* liked it, even if he was a little barbed in his judgement. "The Hawaii-born cat in the white trilby hat undoubtedly has chutzpah, even if he and his songs are infrequently as entertaining as the lavish spectacle that unfolds around him tonight beneath a giant disco ball," he wrote. "Much of this show's immense watchability derives from Mars' eight virtuoso backing musicians, the Hooligans. During 'Treasure', they assemble for some James Brown and the Famous Flames-style formation dancing; come 'Runaway Baby', they wind and grind comedically as Mars declares: 'We got you ladies.' At one point in 'Marry You' there are so many musicians hurtling around clutching horns and guitars, it's like a bomb alert at a big band rehearsal."

David Pollock in *The Independent* was positive. "Amidst a show that never flags from an often bewildering level of hyperactivity, trying on various tones and styles for size through its 90 minutes, the song ['Runaway Baby'] is perhaps the purest example of what Mars… gets right with his music. It borrows from the past and offers a very contemporary pop thrill all at once," he wrote.

Bruno turned 28 when he was in London, an event marked by a concert at the O2 attended by Coldplay's Chris Martin and the Beckham family, followed by a visit from the Beckhams backstage and drinks with Chris. Meanwhile, he was being credited for the disco music revival as one of a number of artists harking back to that long-gone era, the others being Justin Timberlake, Daft Punk and Robin Thicke, alongside DJ producers including David Guetta, Skrillex and DJ Cassidy.

But not everyone was totally positive. Bruno's image when he started out had been close to squeaky clean and that had changed. Lachie Chapman, of the equally squeaky clean group the Overtones, was one person who had her reservations. "Music can be so provocative now," he told the *Daily Star*. "Boundaries are there to be pushed. I love Bruno Mars but look at the lyrics to 'Gorilla'. He's gone from singing 'Marry You' to talking about getting high on coke and humping like a gorilla." He had indeed, but then Bruno was aware that he had to take risks and he couldn't allow his image to stagnate. And the songs were selling well. Bruno certainly wasn't worried about it: at the MTV Europe Music Awards in Amsterdam that November, he brought a pole dancer on the stage when he performed 'Gorilla'. But then this was Amsterdam. The red light district was nearby. He also won an award for Best Song.

Lachie's views weren't shared by everyone, anyway. Towards the end of 2013, Bruno became part of a select group of musicians who were paid an absolute fortune to sing at a private party. In Bruno's case, this entailed being paid nearly £1 million to perform five songs at the bar mitzvah of Russian oligarch Len Blavatnik's daughter: this worked out at about £180,000 a song. He and his entourage were to be flown to New York by private jet, too.

And despite his occasional rauchiness, he was often deemed to be family friendly, too. One report discovered that Bruno's 'Just The Way You Are' and Adele's 'Someone Like You' were the most popular songs for parents with young children, an issue because many young children enjoyed singing along with the charts and parents now chose to sing these songs rather than traditional lullabies. And so it was official. Bruno ended the year not just the favourite of traditional audiences, but also the favourite of babies and their parents. All in all, it had been quite a year, veering from highs to lows, but with Bruno's star steadily in the ascendant. He had become one of the biggest names – and voices – of his generation, selling records in their millions and becoming a global sensation. But he was still near the beginning of his career. The best was yet to come.

Chapter 13

Thank You For The Music

The Bruno effect was beginning to spread. Of course, Bruno wasn't the only musical member of the family – all of his brothers and sisters had grown up around music as well, and they were starting to find some success too. In early 2013, four of his sisters, Presley (named after the King, natch), Tiara, Jaime and Tahiti, got together to form a band, the Lylas, which stood for Love You Like A Sister. It was something of a double-edged sword, being Bruno's sisters: as Tiara pointed out, yes, people paid attention to them because they were Bruno's sisters, but at the same time they were compared to him. He was by now an established superstar; they were just starting out. They could quite easily have suffered badly in the comparison.

In April it was announced that they would be the stars of a new television reality show on WE TV: "The Lylas are fierce, independent women, leaving their home – and in some cases their relationships and kids – for a chance at pursuing their love of music," WE TV's Lauren Gellert said in a statement. "Their story is one filled with all of the drama and chaos that comes from making a major life change, with the added spice of doing it alongside your sisters." And having a famous brother, of course.

There was some excitement at the news that Bruno's sisters were to branch out, with their first single being a number called 'Come Back'. It did moderately well although it failed to make much of a splash. It didn't hurt that the girls were as good looking as Bruno: all signed a modelling contract with Robinson's Department Store in the Philippines. They were also almost immediately embroiled in controversy when one of the girl bands on *The X Factor* attempted to adopt the name the Lylas: after a row the newcomers were forced to change their name to Fifth Harmony.

As with Bruno, there was considerable interest in the family dynamic. "We probably fight more than we get along," said Tahiti. "But because we're sisters, it lasts two minutes. It's sisterly fights." Two also had children: Tahiti was mother to two boys, Nyjah Music, then three, and Zyah Rhythm, two. Jaime, the oldest of the sisters, who was actually born a cousin but adopted into the Hernandez family, also has two boys, Marley, 14, and Jaimo, seven. She had also established the global charity group Mothers About Making Amends (Mama Earth) five years ago to promote giving to humanitarian, environmental and arts causes.

There was some disappointment when the show started to air, as Bruno wasn't actually present – his second album came out just as filming began and he was rather busy promoting that – but there was no shortage of drama. Filmed over a tumultuous year, it portrayed the women moving from Hawaii to LA, engaged in fights with their management and coping with the tragic and unexpected death of their mother. It was revealed that Bruno would offer them advice – "We pretty much ignore it," said Tiara. "Because he's our brother and that's what sisters do."

But the girls all came across well. Jaime cited their mother, Bernadette, as their inspiration: "Our family did a show called the

Love Notes about doo-wop music, and our mom would always make us harmonise," she said. "Our mom would say, 'We're going to sing 'Going To The Chapel'. She would give us each parts and we would sing along." And of Presley, she remarked, "She's definitely the observant one of the group. She's listening, but people tend to underestimate that. She might be quiet at first but when she finally talks, you're going to listen." In all, they came across as a fiery lot, quite a way removed from their little brother's laid-back persona.

The girls had in fact been so close to their mother that the first name they chose for themselves was the Bernadettes, and it was shortly after they started filming that Bernadette so suddenly and shockingly died. The very first scene of the opening episode showed them getting tattoos in their mother's honour. "It's the kind of thing that can drive you apart or bring you together," Tiara told the *New York Daily News*. "It brought us together. I wake up in the morning and I have like 50 text messages from my sisters. We text each other all morning saying, 'See you in the studio' and when we leave the studio we start texting again. 'I'm going home now.' 'I'm going out to dinner now.' 'I'm taking a shower now.' It's exhausting sometimes. But that's how close we all are."

The show opened in November 2013 to somewhat muted viewer reaction. Will the girls emulate their brother's success? Probably not, if truth be told. But only time will tell.

Another successful member of that enormously musical family was, of course, Eric Hernandez, Bruno's older brother, who played the drums as a member of the Hooligans and had already to a certain extent made it, while the girls were still starting out. Remarkably, there seemed to be no sibling rivalry whatsoever: Eric was happy for his little brother to be the centre of attention, while he stayed in the background on the drums. He was a little older turning professional than Bruno had been, not going pro until he was a full 10 years old, but like Bruno, he had been playing music pretty much all his life.

Like Bruno, it was the boys' father, Peter, who sparked their interest at the outset. "Absolutely!" Eric told thedrumshop.co.uk. "As you know he was a percussionist, when I was growing up he had steady gigs six nights a week, as a percussionist before the Love Notes Show. He would take me to his gigs, and if you're familiar with Hawaii, you know there's hula dancing and Tahitian dancing, so they have these percussion instruments called toeres and every night I'd get to go with him to the gig I would sit under the stand of the instrument. However, I was always fixated on the traps drummer, I was watching the drummer the whole time, and he knew that and figured that I wasn't into percussion. So at four he finally bought me a drum set, and it's been that ever since!"

Eric had not, however, had the benefits of a formal education in music, something that he had come to regret. "It's all self-taught," he continued. "I'm not proud of that, [well,] to an extent I am. What happened was for me being thrown into an opportunity to be a professional musician at 10, in a family business, gave me a taste of that life. Therefore, I wouldn't say I'd made it in my mind, but was like 'OK I'm already doing this'. I developed as years went by, I got better and better, and so at the time it was 'I'm too cool to go to jazz-band class or take even high-school marching band'. I regret that now, and I wish I had taken those courses, but if truth be told, at the time I really didn't have time. It was either get my school work done, study and go work at night, get off at 11pm, sleep then get up for school again, so there really wasn't time for the after-school stuff, but I sure wish I did it. I sure wish I did college education and pursue music and I'd tell anybody to do that. Being self-taught is cool, but definitely everybody has different ideas and you learn from that. I mean I have lessons now, I'm behind the curve. Fortunately I've got a good gig and have always had good gigs so I'm not complaining, but if I could do it over again, I would definitely take some higher education class!"

Not that it seemed to be holding him back now. As with his sisters, the comparison could have gone either way between Bruno and Eric, but it appeared to be working out remarkably well. And it meant that Bruno had a strong support team around him, not just musically, but emotionally, as well. Now that it was all coming together, he was spending a serious amount of time out on the road, and so to have a brother and a best friend to chill out with when the crowds had gone home was a huge bonus. It was in everyone's best interest for this particular arrangement to work out well – and it did.

It helped that the brothers understood one another because they were, after all, both committed musicians. Professional respect was evident in their relationship, alongside the ties of a familial past. Would Eric ever branch out on his own, as Philip was to do, of which more below? Probably not, was the truthful answer, but matters were working out so well he didn't want to. There are drawbacks to being in the full glare of the spotlight and it was a good life to be out on the road and yet stay relatively anonymous.

At any rate, to listen to Eric tell it, it was clear the arrangement was working for everyone. "It's great!" he said when asked what it was like to work with his brother. "At the end of the day if you have family that gets along who wouldn't want to have this type of experience with a family member? Fortunately for him and for me, his business, his music, has been successful. His music has become my vehicle for travelling the world, seeing and playing in beautiful places, playing in front of thousands of people, being on TV. I'm 10 years older than him, and I came out to California to pursue my dreams, he followed and now we're living them together. I mean at the same time, sometimes it sucks that he's my boss and he's my little bother and I wanna punch him out! Ha ha! But, he's smart, he knows what he's talking about!"

Whatever the truth about the breakdown of the Fernandez parents' marriage and their subsequent divorce, they'd done something right to breed that kind of attitude. For Eric to be able to accept the situation in the way he did required a certain amount of maturity, which he quite clearly had in spades. It would have been galling for many siblings to see their brother make it in such a spectacular way, but that Eric was able to see that Bruno's success was affording him opportunities he wouldn't have had otherwise was a testament both to the strength of their relationship and to the ties within the family as a whole. It was a similar setup to that of the sisters: the family members could be feisty, but ultimately it was all about family and being able to stick up for one another. And that was also a bonus for Bruno out there in that competitive world. He had someone to watch his back.

And anyway, the schedule was so hectic that it was a relief to have Eric around to help share the burden. "When we played Carlisle we were on tour and we left the United States after a show in Arizona, flew to Newcastle, did the Radio 1 Big Weekend Show the next day and flew the next morning back on tour," explained Bruno. "So we went from the West Coast here, did that one hit, came all the way back and got right back into it. That's common so sometimes you're like 'Where am I?'"

Something else the brothers were able to share was the sheer delight at what was happening to them. It all still seemed so new and unreal, because although both had been working in the industry for years before Bruno made it, at the same time success, when it came, was seemingly overnight. All these new experiences were affecting both of them, even if one was much more famous than the other, and both were equally thrilled at everything coming their way. When Eric was asked what was his most memorable gig to date, he replied, "Probably *Saturday Night Live* because that was my first TV show and that was also my dream as a kid. I used to watch it every Saturday religiously and see my favorite bands and I used to say that I want to play on that train station set. To me, playing *SNL* was like I was making it in the business, and the Grammys, last year's Grammys, was so killer because the performance was flawless, the set looked awesome, and it was probably the best TV mix we've had. Playing on TV can be tough and live sound doesn't always transpose properly, but that I can watch! That performance on TV or a laptop, you can hear all the different parts and it makes me proud of that performance." It was many a childhood dream to play *Saturday Night Live*, of course, and all the sweeter that two people who had shared that dream as youngsters were actually experiencing the reality together. Both were enjoying themselves more than they had ever formerly thought they'd be able to.

But it was hard work, for Bruno, Eric and everyone involved. Their schedules were now packed tight as sardines in a tin and a phenomenal amount of planning had to be done in advance. That was the other downside of fame and success – everyone wanted a part of you and if you wanted to stay ahead in the game you barely had time to draw breath.

One of the reasons they operated so well together was that Eric was able to be selfless enough to see that the needs of his little brother were paramount. Again, the closeness of the family unit, to say nothing of Eric's own amiable character, helped. But there was a certain degree of pragmatism in there, too. After all, Bruno was the successful one and so it was in the interests of the entire family to ensure that he stayed that way. For if he was doing well, then the chances became all the greater that everyone who worked with him would do well, too. The entertainment industry was littered with those who became successful on the back of their siblings, and so it was logical to promote Bruno's interests. Eric did work for other people in the industry too, but was in no doubt where his loyalties were.

"Bruno comes first," Eric said. "I did a few spots between Taio Cruz and Bruno, but that was when Bruno was doing promo, so I had time to juggle both. Now that Bruno's record has progressed and had its success, I haven't had time to juggle. I could take some gigs when I'm down [from touring], but I've chosen to work on myself, to practise and spend time with my family. Right now Bruno is the priority and as long as we're successful as a unit, it's gonna stay the priority." It was a very sensible attitude to have.

And like Bruno, Eric had become wearily aware of quite how difficult it was to make it in the music industry in LA. For Bruno himself, of course, it had all finally come good, but both brothers had had to fight every inch of the way just to get themselves heard. It could be dispiriting – LA was the city of many a broken dream and Eric sometimes sounded on the verge of disillusionment. But then, courtesy of Bruno, he was on the edge of great success and was sensible enough to know that while it might be hard to make the breakthrough, it was still worth the fight.

"Tough," he said, when he was asked how he found the LA music scene. "It's competitive, you got a lot of great players out here. You got Musician's Institute here too. But there is opportunity. When I first moved out here, there was a music magazine that posted want ads and I found a band that was signed to RCA Records and was seeking a drummer. I did an audition and got the gig, and we did tour rehearsals and were gonna tour with Duncan Sheek and Big Head Todd and Susana Hoffs. Somewhere their deal went south so I came home and started to get back into the circuit playing all the clubs in LA. The gigs are out there, you have to hustle. Nowadays you really have to be a package deal and have a look. The scene is good and it's hard as hell, but if this is what you want to do then you get yourself right in the middle of it. That's what I did, I put myself here. It took 15 years but I never stopped." And now, after all that time and effort, success was coming his way.

He was not alone. The Bruno effect wasn't just rubbing off on his family, but on close friends and colleagues, too. In September 2013, Bruno's fellow Smeezington Philip Lawrence became the latest to benefit, when he released his solo debut, *Letters I Never Sent*, also on Atlantic, Bruno's label. Could the magic repeat itself? It was hard to say. But Philip had been in a very similar situation to Bruno: he too had always wanted to make it as a solo artist, and given the huge success enjoyed not only by Bruno but also by the Smeezingtons as a whole, now was clearly the right time to try.

There was considerable interest from the music industry. Given that the Smeezingtons had already produced one superstar, could another possibly be on the cards? Philip began talking about what he had produced and like Bruno, he had a hugely diverse range of musical influences. "It's a collection of the music I like to listen to," Phil told rap-up.com. "I'm a huge fan of folk music. I'm a huge fan of rock music, huge fan of Seal, Billy Joel, singer-songwriter guys. I think I was channelling my inner singer-songwriter with this album." And he agreed the previous few years had been quite something. "It's a rare thing that you not only get to experience this kind of success and the wonderful things that we've been exposed to, but to do it with your boy, to do it with someone you came up with, to do it with someone who equally believes in you, there's a huge sense of camaraderie," he said. "Every day I walk on that stage, we look at each other and go, 'We did it.' It's really, really cool."

The album had in some ways been years in the making. The Smeezingtons worked so well together that they not only inspired one another to make communal work, but to express their individual creativity, too. This had been bubbling in the background, as it were, for a very long time and as so often is the case, exploded out in a great burst of creativity that could no longer be contained. "The title sort of came from... the majority of the songs on the album were recorded back in 2009, around the time Bruno and I were working together pretty heavily and his shuttle was about to take off and I could see his popularity growing," Philip said in another interview, this one with vibe. com. "I thought to myself, 'If I'm ever going to record an album I should probably do it now because who knows when I'm going to have a chance again.' I knew that we were going to be touring and all these wonderful things were going to be happening with him, so ... fast forwarding now to four or five years later they were almost the songs that were never heard. They were like these letters or ideas and songs that were almost never sent, but fortunately now the world can hear them."

The parallels with Bruno didn't stop there. Like Bruno, who has famously said that every song he has ever written is based on some sort of personal experience, Philip too used his own life as a starting point. And here was the real difference in writing for himself rather than other people: the finished product was totally his own. And again, as so many artists before him had found, it was a far more personal statement than anything he had written before. "It was like therapy," he continued. "It was very cathartic for me, because sometimes it's a little rare in popular music to be able to have the freedom to be honest and speak from the heart and talk about issues in your life and try to be an open book. A lot of times that's not the kind of stuff you want to hear on the radio, which is understandable. For me going in to write this album I wanted it to be an honest portrayal of things happening in my life and things I'm struggling with, the good and the bad. It was like a therapy session, it was good to be able to talk about it, sing about, to be able to come face to face with things that I've been through."

Like Bruno, it was not entirely possible to put Philip into any one pigeonhole; he channelled a wide range of musical influences that meant it was hard to pin him down. And although at the time of writing it is still impossible to say if his career would take off like Bruno's, this did offer a promise of longevity that many other artists wouldn't have. It offered the potential to appeal to a wider audience, to switch genres if one went out of fashion and, of course, to manage to continue to surprise. Some of the most successful pop careers have been built on constant reinvention and it looked as if Philip was going to be able to manage to do just that.

Again, as with Bruno, the key lay in all those eclectic childhood influences and the fact that his father had also been in the music industry. "I just think it's a combination of the influences that I've had over the years," Philip went on. "My dad was a DJ back in the seventies. When I was growing up, there was at any given time crates and crates of albums just lying around the house. We were exposed to everything from the Isley Brothers to the Eagles to Led Zeppelin, Billy Joel, Stevie Wonder, and this sort of gumbo melting pot of musicians and artists that we were exposed to helped shape the things that I liked. That's why you'll hear maybe a funk song, or you'll hear a rock song as well. A lot of that is true to what Bruno and I do as well. We try not to be pigeonholed into any kind of style. We work on what moves us."

It was certainly a bonus that the two had each other and Ari to bounce off against. All three had an extremely sharp ear for what worked: after all those years of experience, they were quite as good a judge of what worked, what didn't and what would appeal to the public as anyone else. Philip was clearly excited to be getting his moment in the limelight, though: while the easy-going camaraderie between the three of them had never changed, even when one of them became so very much more famous than the other two, Philip was thrilled that now the spotlight was shining on him.

It had been a struggle to get there, however, and that struggle also manifested itself in the work. Philip said that the song 'Neverland', about the hard times he had suffered in the early years, was the most personal of the lot: "That one chronicled a lot of things that were happening in LA years ago when I was struggling, trying to find my way," he went on. "There's a lot of times in our industry that it's easy to make excuses for not being able to accomplish certain things or find distractions to hide the pain of not being a success whether it be partying or whatever your vice may be. That song is me telling myself to put away the childish things, man up and really focus on what it is that your goals are, and leave this 'never land' place behind. I think that one was more of a true story for me.

"On my album I think the style was just to try to be honest and try to have melodies that are memorable enough for people to have the lyrics resonate with them. I think a lot of times melodies really play a huge part in people remembering what it is you wrote. If you have a really catchy melody, even if they don't immediately understand the lyrics, the more they sing that melody the more they'll adapt the lyrics to that. We tried to pay attention to that on my album and of course we always do that with Bruno as well. If I had to describe the style it would be to try to make it as memorable as possible." It was the attitude the Smeezingtons regularly applied to their work.

Plenty of other, less high-profile people benefitted from the Bruno effect as well. There were all the people behind the scenes, who worked on his various tours and as Bruno got more successful, so did they. One of these was Cory FitzGerald, one of the co-designers on the Moonshine Jungle tour, a massively ambitious undertaking, festooned with a giant disco ball and nods to the seventies, eighties and nineties – in other words, a reference to Bruno's own musical influences. "I was 12 years old and doing a summer theatre program when I quickly realised that

I enjoyed being backstage rather than on it," Cory FitzGerald, who worked with the well established live design expert, LeRoy Bennett, told *Total Production International*. "The rest as they say, is history. We started working with Bruno in 2011 designing his Hooligans in Wondaland tour. There were a variety of different paths we went down, but ultimately the idea was to create a world where the band could play their wide range of songs and really own the stage for the whole performance. LeRoy and I worked very closely with Bruno to create the show.

"The needs of the stage and band helped dictate a lot of the spacing on the stage, and the look and feel was a concept that morphed into what it is today based on a lot of back and forth ideas. Bruno is very hands-on and has a unique and clear vision of what he's looking for. I like to use the lights to really capture the dynamics of the music and play along with the songs, just like the musicians do. It's all about expanding on what they are doing in the venue, and giving the audience a visual show to match the energy on stage. Like many shows and artists, Moonshine Jungle is an extension of Bruno himself. His energy and talent are showcased every night on that stage, and we get to help to magnify that. We were tasked with creating a world for Bruno and his band to inhabit. Bruno has a lot of sounds and pushes past a lot of genres, so he needed an environment that would accommodate all his music. The lighting fixtures help a lot with that."

Of course all these men were well established anyway, and would have done well in their chosen careers whatever had happened to Bruno, but the fact was that his success had ripples. The better he did, the better everyone surrounding him did, which meant it was in the best interests of everyone to produce the best work that they could. And they did. Bruno's hands-on interest in every aspect of the tour made him a popular artist to work with, as well – no doubt a by-product of his laid-back Hawaiian charm.

And so what of Ari Levine, the Smeezington's back-room boy? He shows none of the desire to come to the front of the stage that the others have, but equally, his name and his reputation have been made. And he took it as seriously as anyone – this was work. It was business and nothing could change that. Once they had had their first taste of success, they could have gone for a much grander studio and surroundings, but that was not the way they were going to play it, having already succeeded on their own terms.

"We like the studio as it is," he told soundonsound back in 2011 (he has not done many interviews since, preferring, as he himself says it, to remain in the background). "We're not planning to change anything. The studio is not too big, so there is not much room to expand. And we don't want to go somewhere else. This place has a lot of character. It has a really great work vibe – we are here to work, not to sit around and watch TV and eat candy. I'll join Bruno and Phil for a couple of weeks of their US tour, and we'll spend some time writing. I'll then come back here and will finish up these tracks. I also just did a song with Taio Cruz, I'm working with a band called the Rescues, and I just did four songs with an artist named John West. So I do a lot of production here in my studio, on my own. As I said, I have no desire to go on stage or be famous. I simply plan to continue working with the Smeezingtons and work by myself as a producer."

Hugely in demand across the industry, he too has been a beneficiary of the Bruno effect – as has much of the wider world. For Bruno's influence was continuing to spread.

Chapter 14

His Just Deserts

It had been a meteoric rise. In just three years, Bruno had gone from being talented back-room boy to global superstar and the rewards were really beginning to flood in. He had sold 40 million singles worldwide, 12 and a half million of which were for 'Just The Way You Are'. He had sold six million albums, become the best-selling digital artist in 2011 and had won one award after another, including Best International Male Solo Artist at the 2012 BRIT Awards. It wasn't just fame and recognition that had come his way, either: Bruno had become a very wealthy man. But he was displaying a social conscience, as well, beginning to support charities and lend his name to good causes. The world had given him a lot – and he was intent on giving something back.

Indeed, for someone who had been given so much so quickly, Bruno remained remarkably level headed. It is no surprise that many young stars, who go from having nothing to having a huge amount, end up running out of control, but Bruno was not one of them. His fortune is now in the tens of millions, probably at least $15 million by the end of 2013. His biggest outlay to date has been an eminently sensible one: he paid $3.2 million for a very slinky bachelor pad in the Laurel Canyon area on Mulholland Drive in the Hollywood Hills. The three-bedroom one-level house, which dates from the middle of the twentieth century, has been described as "magazine worthy", with radiant floor heating, Miele appliances, Swarovski crystal lighting and spectacular floor to ceiling retractable glass walls which look out over amazing mountain and city views. A huge 11-foot entry dominates the building, while it also boasts a gym, massage facilities, a steam shower and a dry sauna. Behind the house there's a luxurious swimming pool and outdoor sound system. Elsewhere on the property are parking facilities for up to 10 cars. In other words, it was the perfect home for a pop star, with neighbours attesting to Bruno's new status including George Clooney and Pamela Anderson.

In all, Bruno was seen as pretty frugal in pop star terms, but he had not forgotten what it was like to have nothing at all. And with the insecurity felt by just about every entertainer, there was always the lurking fear that it could all go again. But this was, after all, the man who had written 'Billionaire', which encouraged a good deal of curiosity about whether this mirrored his own attitude towards money. It didn't, but he did know what it was like to be hard up. "The inspiration behind 'Billionaire' was, I was tired of spending half my day worrying about what I can and can't spend on whatever," he said in one interview with *Forbes* magazine. "I wouldn't have to worry about, you know, 'I can't afford to get breakfast, so I'll wait until lunchtime to eat.' If I was a billionaire, none of that would matter. I'd be eating diamond cereal." Despite this, however, some critics have claimed that Bruno had no right to be singing about wanting to be a billionaire, because he was already very rich, thus totally missing the point that Bruno wrote it when he was actually pretty poor. And while he was wealthy by everyday standards, he still had a long way to go before amassing the hundred million-odd portfolios of some of the more established stars.

However, and admirably, Bruno is well aware of his good fortune and has been working to give something back. He supports a number of youth-related charities, such as Candie's Foundation, a non-profit organisation that educates teenagers about parenthood and the repercussions of a teen pregnancy. Bruno came from a background in which he saw at first hand very young people getting pregnant and the devastating effect it can have on their lives. Amongst other initiatives, he performed at a gala for the organisation in 2011.

Bruno is also a part of Musicians on Call, an organisation comprising 34 supporters that brings live and recorded music to patients in hospitals and health-care facilities. It believes that music can promote and complement the healing process for patients as well as their families and Bruno has been known to attend health-care facilities to entertain. Other causes he supports include the Red Cross, the Rainforest Foundation and DoSomething.

In March 2011, after the tragic Japanese tsunami and earthquake, Bruno was one of 38 artists – others included Madonna, Lady Gaga, Justin Bieber and Beyoncé – to contribute to a compilation album called *Songs For Japan*, the proceeds of which would go to the Red Cross. The description on iTunes was as follows: "As Japan recovers from the devastating earthquake and tsunami that struck March 11th, the world's top recording artists respond to the tragedy with a benefit album. The 38 tracks include some of the biggest hits, featuring an exclusive remix of Lady Gaga's 'Born This Way', along with original versions of Katy Perry's 'Firework', Bruno Mars' 'Talking To The Moon', Adele's 'Make You Feel My Love' and more. Apple, the labels, and the artists are donating their proceeds to the Japanese Red Cross."

In fact, Bruno regularly supported the Red Cross when tragic events took place. In May 2011, after a tornado had devastated certain parts of the United States, Bruno auctioned off some memorabilia to raise money for the cause, with this notice on Facebook: "Bruno is auctioning off some signed & rare items to benefit the victims of the massive tornadoes in Alabama. All proceeds of this auction will go to the Alabama Tornado Disaster Relief Fund via The American Red Cross. Anything you can do to help would be most appreciated!" He was using his fame to aid a good cause.

His support for the Rainforest Foundation saw him teamed with one of the biggest stars of them all. In April 2012, Bruno and a host of others gathered in New York's Carnegie Hall, where they played a concert entitled Songs From The Silver Screen. The show opened with Meryl Streep, Sting, James Taylor and Elton John singing 'If I Only Had A Brain' from *The Wizard Of Oz*: Meryl dressed as Dorothy, Sting wore a tin hat and Elton John sported furry paws – and ruby slippers. It was Elton with whom Bruno was partnered in what was generally agreed to be one of the standout moments of the evening, a duet of the much covered 'Unchained Melody': Bruno was alongside a man who had been in the entertainment spotlight for decades and yet he still managed to hold his own. He also sang alongside Jennifer Hudson, again effortlessly holding the room: "Bruno Mars was rocking out the house and alongside him was Jennifer Hudson," proclaimed examiner.com. "Known individually for their talent in music, the two artists coming together on the same stage had fans elated. Those audience members watching the concert live at Carnegie Hall and using Twitter to relay messages to their friends called the two performing 'epic' and 'overwhelmingly delightful.'"

The *Hollywood Reporter* certainly approved. "Mars got some of the biggest cheers of the evening, first for his soaring duet with John on 'Unchained Melody' and again for his hip-swivelling 'Jailhouse Rock'," wrote Frank Scheck. "Not everything worked. Taylor, who seems temperamentally unsuited for the angst of

'Ol' Man River', somehow managed to turn it into a feel-good song. On the other hand, John, informing the crowd that 'It has become a custom at these shows for me to humiliate myself,' good-naturedly fulfilled his mandate by singing 'Diamonds Are A Girl's Best Friend' while waving his rock-covered digits and bumping and grinding with Channing Tatum." But more to the point, Bruno had not been overshadowed by these giants of the entertainment industry. If he could hold his own with Elton John, then he could hack it with just about anyone in the world.

Nor was that all. Bruno took part in the inaugural Hilarity for Charity event in 2012 to raise funds for the Alzheimer's Association, performing a jokey cover of Celine Dion's 'My Heart Will Go On' and, with the other performers, signing a ukulele which was used in a giveaway. October 2012 saw the release of *Rhythms Del Mundo: Africa*, the latest project from Artists Project Earth, an organisation that aims to raise awareness and funds for climate change and disaster relief projects. The vocals of stars including Coldplay, Eminem, Red Hot Chili Peppers, Beyoncé, Fleet Foxes, Mumford & Sons and Bruno, combined with the instrumentation of high-profile African musicians like Toumani Diabaté and Rokia Traoré, all featured on the album. In March 2013, he put in a very creditable performance of 'Let's Dance' for Comic Relief.

And of course, as his fame grew ever greater, he was increasingly in demand. In September 2013, alongside Macklemore & Ryan Lewis, Trey Songz and various others, Bruno customised all-white Chuck Taylor sneakers as part of the In Their Shoes initiative, which raises money for the National Breast Cancer Foundation. Other designers included the Black Keys, Red Hot Chili Peppers, Skrillex and Charli XCX, and the shoes were put up for auction on eBay. This was all done with a great deal of good humour. It was also a sign that Bruno had joined the great and good.

But it wasn't all do-gooding. Along the way, as he has refined his image, Bruno has become associated with certain brands and looks and a great deal of attention was paid to the way he looked and dressed himself, as he began to turn into a style icon. Bruno tends to do casual chic: he is often seen in Levi's skinny 511 jeans when he is out and abut, preserving those razor sharp suits for the stage. He likes Ray-Ban Original Wayfarer 2140 sunglasses, Converse by John Varvatos rubberised chucks sneakers (hence his charitable contribution to the cause was particularly apt), Ray-Ban RX 5121 eyeglasses (when he's not wearing the sunnies), Obey Burlington jacket and a Rolex day date Presidential wristwatch with champagne stick dial, one of Bruno's few real extravagances. His naturally slender frame lends itself well to being a clothes horse, but it all cultivated the image of a sophisticate about town.

This image was further enhanced when it was announced that Bruno would wear designs by the Italian fashion greats Domenico Dolce and Stefano Gabbana when he set off on his Moonshine Jungle tour. Dolce & Gabbana had worked with some of the true musical greats in the past: they created Madonna's costumes for the Girlie Show tour, and had also dressed Mary J Blige, Kylie Minogue and Beyoncé. The fashion house put out a statement: "Bruno's style and music are so eclectic that oftentimes we have taken inspiration directly from his work to create looks that were at the same time in line with his very personal taste, as well as with the DNA of Dolce & Gabbana," it said. "With time, we have managed to establish with him a relationship of absolute faith in each other and mutual trust, that allows us to create and work together in an atmosphere of complete harmony." What this boiled down to was super sharp stage attire, teaming red suits with leopard-skin shirts and having Bruno stand out, even more than previously, from the crowd.

And of course, there is the ever present fedora. This became so ubiquitous that on his 27th birthday, popdust.com published 27 pictures of him wearing a fedora, citing a number of reasons that he wears it so often: it makes him seem deep and introspective before he opens his mouth, it signifies he's up for anything, it earns him the respect of his peers (this was illustrated by a picture of him embracing Elton John), it helps shield his eyes from the harsh lights of the stage – and it contains his sweat. Not to let it rest there, the website then ran a series of pictures in which Bruno combined his fedora with sunglasses. It also, of course, gave him a signature look that had people talking about him. A very wearable marketing tool.

He drives a 2012 CTS Sport Sedan and favours designers such as Hugo Boss and Armani. He sometimes, albeit less frequently, favours the more blinging style of a rapper, all gold chains, gold bracelets and gold rings, although this is not his usual look. He did, however, combine an awful lot of bling with a leopard-skin shirt for his appearance on the front cover of *Rolling Stone* in May 2013, in which he gave an unusually revealing interview, talking for the first time about how the poorer portion of his childhood made him appreciate his wealth and fame all the more as an adult. To make the point, the magazine labelled Bruno "Pop's Golden Child".

Although still a relative newcomer to the music scene, Bruno has already exerted a far greater cultural reach than would normally have been expected, thanks in no small part to the fact that he writes the songs as well as singing them. With a tenor three-octave vocal range, the most frequent comparison is with the young Michael Jackson, before it all went so horribly wrong. The critic Jim Farber noticed this: writing a review of one of the shows in *The New York Daily News* he said, "Mars' voice enhances the image. It has the purity, cream and range of mid-period Michael Jackson, right before the fall. Like the King of Pop, Mars pines for the prerock-era role of the pure entertainer, a classic song-and-dance man. To enhance his all-in-one-approach, he took time to peel out a guitar solo and pound on the drums. He inhabited the glad-handing part so winningly, it hardly seemed to matter that the show wasn't big on risk or depth. Mars reached for more emotion in the few slower numbers. But his forte remains energy and engagement, embracing pop at its most colourful and pleasing."

He was versatile, too, moving easily from one genre to another, as Jon Caramanica pointed out in *The New York Times*. Bruno had recently admitted to his past as an infant Elvis impersonator, to say nothing of all the other musicians he'd channelled across the years and it could well have been that that made him able to leap so nimbly from one style to the next. "Still, there's something to be said for learning a wide repertory at a young age, and also to feel no shame in people-pleasing," he wrote. "It's made Mr. Mars, 24, one of the most versatile and accessible singers in pop, with a light, soul-influenced voice that's an easy fit in a range of styles, a universal donor. There's nowhere he doesn't belong."

Indeed, Bruno's ability to write and sing in so many styles cropped up over and over again. "The 24-year-old shows his range, promise, tastes and talents on the record. Working with his writing-producing team known collectively as the Smeezingtons, Mars (born Peter Hernandez in Hawaii) offers up a little reggae, a little rock, and lots of catchy pop hooks," wrote a critic in a review of his first album in The News. "Most of all, he's romantic, singing about love, devotion and the perfect girl on most of the album's tracks. He's sexy with it like D'Angelo on the reggae-tinged 'Our First Time', sweet on 'Just The Way You Are' and the equally poppy 'Marry You', and sassy on the groovy, guitar-heavy 'Runaway Baby'."

Bruno's own take on it was that the early struggles had enabled him to learn his craft. "It opened my eyes. I was able to learn so much before putting out my first album. I got to work with other artists, and it laid the groundwork for me to be ready and put some real songs together," he said in an interview with Kevin C Johnson in *St Louis Today*. "For years I had been getting rejected and rejected and rejected. I was like, 'Is this going to happen?' Then everything took off."

It did, and this time round Bruno was able to deal with it properly. The combination of childhood influences and adult experience had gelled, and with that came the possibility of a much longer career than many musicians could expect to have. To be stuck in one genre is to risk nearing a sell-by date, whereas if you get to the end of one phase of your career and are able to move to the next, it makes for much greater longevity. "It's easier when you understand more about what you're doing," Bruno continued. "It's like a football player knowing the rule book in and out and knowing the sizes of the pads you wear when you go into the field. You have to know every detail about your craft, and when I was younger I didn't know. And I'm still learning every day."

Like the critics, he was well aware that his music fell into various different categories – indeed, he positively relished it now. Over and over again he'd been vindicated, while those record bosses from the early days who had had so much trouble classifying him had been proved utterly wrong. Bruno was thoughtful on the subject of the first album: "'Nothin' On You' had a Motown vibe, 'Billionaire' was a reggae acoustic-guitar-driven song, though one of my favourites is the CeeLo song. I don't think anyone else could've sung that song," he continued. "And there's 'Just The Way You Are'. If you know my story, you know I love all different genres of music."

There was also a strong reggae beat to a lot of his output. This, according to Bruno, was a direct result of what was popular in his home state and what he had grown up listening to himself. "In Hawaii some of the biggest radio stations are reggae," he told the *New York Daily News*. "The local bands are heavily influenced by Bob Marley. That music brings people together. It's not urban music or pop music. It's just songs. That's what makes it cross over so well. The song comes first."

He was also asked about 'The Lazy Song', given that Bruno's output proved him to be anything but idle himself. His reply was revealing, given that he compared himself (not in an egotistical way) to one of the biggest bands of them all. "I hope my body of work proves I'm not [lazy]," he said. "That song just came out of the studio. We were trying to make a song that was better than the Beatles. We were trying to be magical and historic. After five hours, it all turned to rubbish. The frustration got to me and I said, 'Today I don't feel like doing anything at all.' That opened up everyone's eyes. When you're overshooting, you get the worst work. When you're relaxed, you have your best. I'm a light kind of guy."

Well, in part at least. Most of Bruno's music is indeed very light-hearted, but not all. His friend and colleague Philip Lawrence has said in the past, "What people don't know is that there's a darker underbelly to Bruno Mars," and that is undoubtedly true. 'Grenade', 'Liquor Store Blues' and 'Talking To The Moon' detail failed relationships, heavy drinking and drug taking and other self-destructive traits, while Bruno caused serious controversy with songs like 'Gorilla' and its very explicit content. But then again, it would have been surprising if Bruno had not had a darker side. He'd been bullied at school, seen his parents' marriage breakup, been dropped at the beginning of his career, had to endure the pain of his mother's death and generally suffered the slings and arrows of outrageous fortune that are the burden we all must bear. Bruno was not, after all, a little teenage star; he was an adult who had already lived a little. Of course he had a darker side.

Plaudits for Bruno have been rolling in all across the industry. *Rolling Stone*, no less, classed him at number 35 of their list of greatest live acts now: quite a compliment given that the likes of

Bruce Springsteen, Madonna and Leonard Cohen were also on the list. "Anyone from the age of five to 95 can walk out of a Bruno Mars concert feeling like the show was designed just for them," they said. "Mars walks the old-school walk (occasionally in James Brown's funky shoes) and talks the sexy talk (sometimes in Prince-like come-ons), but he also nails the hits, leads a super-energetic nine-piece soul band, and rips a mean drum solo." Bruno was also one of the youngest artists in the list, highlighting how far and how fast he'd come on.

Indeed, all the industry standards loved him. *Billboard*, the music industry standard, was similarly effusive when reviewing his Moonshine Jungle tour: "Don't let the perfectly coiffed hair and easy-going smile fool you: as his 87-date Moonshine Jungle world tour gets underway – the Philadelphia show was the run's second stop, after beginning in Washington DC on Saturday night – Mars has become a stone-cold hit machine who has rattled off a staggering amount of ubiquitous singles over the course of two albums and a few extracurricular appearances," wrote Jason Lipshutz. "He is an efficient, impeccable star that has thrown a bunch of timeless influences into a blender and jammed his finger down on the 'high' button." Efficient, impeccable and timeless? All this about a man who until relatively recently was almost completely unknown.

The Michael Jackson parallels cannot be overestimated – of all the myriad influences upon him, it was Michael who influenced Bruno more than anyone. "I feel like he set the bar for artists," he told the *Daily Record*. "Any artist, I don't care what genre you do, you should always aspire to be like Michael Jackson. Because the details, the attention to detail he did on everything he did, everything he was a part of, you can look at what made him so iconic, the glove, the hat, the dancing, the music videos, the way he sang when he sang, everything he did was Michael Jackson, and he just kind of stamped that on the world."

It was a lesson Bruno himself had very much taken on board. It wasn't just about the music: it was about absolutely everything, from presentation to interpretation. Michael's attention to detail was second to none and Bruno wanted to be the same. "It's one thing to buy the song, like the song, like the lyrics, like the production, it's another thing to see the artist perform that song, that's why Michael Jackson is the best," he went on. "To see him do it, to see whatever it is, the artistic way he brought it to life live, and paint a whole other picture and I feel like it was very important when you hear this album. I want people to be like, I've got to go see this show. It's going to be a good show." They were doing just that. His consummate professionalism meant that audiences were flocking to see him all across the world.

And just like Michael Jackson before him, Bruno took the very wise decision to work with the best people in the industry and it showed. Apart from his fellow Smeezingtons and his band the Hooligans, Bruno is surrounded by people who have helped him fulfill his creative potential. One of these is the music video director Cameron Duddy, with whom Bruno has made a handful of videos reflecting seventies and eighties style. These included 'Locked Out Of Heaven', 'When I Was Your Man' and 'Treasure'. Yet again Bruno's childhood was exerting its influence over his career, this time round by tapping into a note of nostalgia, a ploy that served him very well.

From early on, Bruno has been aware that he is difficult to categorise and that this has turned into one of his strengths. "I know a lot of artists say this, but it's hard to put myself in a box," he said in an interview with *Entertainment Weekly* way back in 2010. "I just write songs that I strongly believe in and that are coming from a special place. There's no tricks. I don't have mascara on on one eye. It's honesty. If you like 'Nothin' On You' and you like 'Billionaire', that's what you're going to get.

You're going to get these melodies. And I'm going to be singing the s— out of it."

Bruno has now himself become an influence on other people. He was constantly being asked about his own musical background, the tastes that shaped him and what had contributed to him becoming the musician he was, but now his impact on the music scene was such that he was frequently cited when other artists talked about who was having an effect on them. There were the people he'd worked with directly, of course, just about all of whom he had gone on to overshadow, but now other entertainers were talking about the impact he'd had on them and how much they would like to work with him. Bruno wasn't just a hot property amongst audiences, but amongst his peers as well.

The Jonas Brothers predated Bruno as successful artists by some years, but it was Bruno that Joe Jonas cited when discussing a new album release in 2013, the first for four years. What could the fans expect? "A lot of old school music – not only blues, but soul music and also some dance music that we were listening to," he told *Parade*. "On top of that, there are artists like Bruno Mars and a couple others that are really using a lot of instruments in their live music that they incorporate with the album. That's what we've been trying to do."

Selina Gomez was another one to sing Bruno's praises. "Most recently, I am obsessed with Bruno Mars," she said in an interview with Popcrush in 2013. "He inspires me in everything he does. His style of music, his style in general, the way he performs, the way he carries himself. I just think he's a really strong artist. I'm very excited he's getting all of the recognition he deserves." Bridgit Mendler was another fan, expressing the desire to collaborate with Bruno. By now, of course, his potential collaborators were in a very different position from the way they had been in the past: at the beginning it was Bruno who was the secondary figure. Now stars were queuing up to appear with him.

And the industry which Bruno has dominated has come to reward him in due turn. At the time of writing, Bruno has won 46 awards from 161 nominations and it really all started to kick off in the year of his breakthrough, 2010. That year, Bruno received eight nominations and won two awards, one at the Soul Train Music Awards for Song of the Year, for his collaboration with B.o.B on 'Nothin' On You' and the other at the Z Awards for Best New Artist.

The following year, the nominations and wins began in earnest. In 2011, Bruno received 67 nominations and won 20, including Favourite Pop/Rock Male Artist at the American Music Awards, Best New Act and Best Push at the MTV Video Music Awards, Best International Artist at the BT Digital Music Awards and Breakout Artist and Choice Summer as Male Music Star at the Teen Choice Awards; Best Male Video for 'Just the Way You Are' at MTV Video Music Awards Japan, 'Just The Way You Are' as Top Radio Song at the *Billboard* Music Awards and Best Male Pop Vocal Performance for 'Just The Way You Are' at the Grammy Awards. Nor did he just receive awards at the various events; Bruno often performed, too. At the 2011 MTV Video Music Awards he performed Amy Winehouse's song 'Valerie' as a tribute to the star who died that year; his performance was considered to be one of the highlights of the evening, both for its emotional content and for the sublime showmanship for which Bruno was coming to be known.

In 2012, by now an established star, Bruno received 43 nominations and won 12, including International Male Solo Artist at the Brit Awards; Best International Male at the Echo Awards; Favourite Male Artist at the People's Choice Awards; Best Breaking Act International at the Swiss Music Awards and Best Male Video for 'It Will Rain' at the MTV Video Music Awards Japan. In 2013, Mars received 50 nominations and most are pending.

His work as a producer and songwriter, alongside his production team the Smeezingtons, has also been recognised at the ASCAP's Rhythm & Soul Music Awards with the award for Top Rap Song for the single 'Nothin' On You' and at the Grammy Awards, with two nominations for Producer of the Year, Non-Classical, three nominations for Record of the Year with the songs 'Nothin' On You', 'Grenade' and 'Fuck You' and 'Young, Wild & Free' for Best Rap Song. If Bruno was after recognition, he had well and truly earned it. He was now one of the leading lights of the industry that had refused to recognise his talents for so long.

Chapter 15

Superstar

The year 2013 had been a rollercoaster: total highs and terrible lows. But by the year end, Bruno was in an even stronger position than before. It had been announced that he was to perform at the Super Bowl in February 2014, following the likes of Madonna, Michael Jackson, Black Eyed Peas, Beyoncé, U2, Janet Jackson and Bruce Springsteen, the very aristocracy of rock 'n' roll. In truth though, although Bruno was on the verge of joining the ranks of the greats, there was still a way to go. Hard as it might be to break into the top echelons of the music scene, it was even harder to stay there, and if his was to be a career that really ranked alongside the likes of Michael Jackson, then there was still going to be quite a way to go. Bruno's career had so far lasted years; the aim was to make it last decades.

But the omens were good. In an industry renowned for its competitiveness and backstabbing, Bruno was a popular figure, a perfectionist, certainly, with an eye to detail and a hands-on approach to absolutely everything he did, but not one of the bad guys. He was brimming with confidence, which could sometimes be misinterpreted as arrogance, but he had not allowed success to go to his head. The struggle had been too hard and, courtesy of the cocaine incident, he knew how easy it would be to lose it all again. But Bruno was in it for the long haul and was becoming one of the best-known faces in town. He also continued to give something back to society: in November 2013, he became one of a number of artists to contribute a song to the album *Songs For The Philippines*, which was raising money to help disaster relief after the terrible typhoon had swept through the country.

Certainly, these days, magazines were clamouring to put him on their covers, including that Bible of the rock 'n' roll industry, *Rolling Stone*. With his sharp suits, trademark fedora and shades, Bruno was not only good looking – he was cool. To be associated with him these days was to be associated with someone as hot as the inside of a volcano and it was increasingly common these days for young up-and-coming entertainers to be compared to the great man as "the new Bruno Mars". While this was a constant reminder that there were keen young bods snapping at his heels behind them, it was also a sign that he was totally established in what he did. It hadn't been so long since Bruno was being called "the new Michael Jackson"; he was now himself someone whose status was to be aspired to and, in most cases, not actually gained.

The industry recognized this too. It continued to belatedly make up for taking so long to award Bruno a breakthrough by thrusting awards at him: towards the end of 2013, Bruno was nominated for four Grammy awards, for Record of the Year, Song of the Year and Best Pop Solo Performance for 'When I Was Your Man' and Best Pop Vocal Album for *Unorthodox Jukebox*. 'When I Was Your Man' clearly touched a wider audience as much as it did Bruno and remains one of the most popular of his songs.

Of course, not everyone was ecstatic about Bruno's success. Kanye West, for one, showed distinct signs of the little green monster in a rant recorded by Real Talk NY in November, 2013. "When I went to the MTV Awards, Rick Rubin hit me, he said

'Are you performing at the MTV Awards,'" said Kanye. "I said 'Yeah.' He said 'Look man, just do your **** song and leave. Just do your song and leave. Just do your song and leave.' Cause sure enough I'm sitting down trying, I'm trying to enjoy **** performing and shit... And then they start giving out awards and shit. And Bruno Mars win all the **** awards and shit. You know, I was just thinking about what Rick Rubin told me cause I don't give a fuck about no TV show. But what I care about is if you an artist and you work hard as fuck and the streets say that you deserve that shit then can't no **** networks try to gas everybody up. So, they can sell some [product] with the prettiest **** out."

It was a pretty foul-mouthed rant, and more than a little unfair. Bruno's good looks were certainly no hindrance to his success, but neither were they the reason for it, either. As the industry was finding over and over, he was an exceptionally versatile performer, not only capable of singing and dancing, but playing a multitude of different instruments and writing his own music, too. Fizzing with energy, his stage performances were often downright exciting, while Bruno's ability to communicate with an audience meant that the moment he walked on stage he had them on our side. He was constantly exhorting them to enjoy themselves (they did), to have a little fun (they did that, too), to sit back or indeed stand up and enjoy the ride. The shows had a glamorous element to them as well: all that disco reference might have been a little kitschy at times, but grungy it was not. Bruno loved the high camp of the seventies and eighties and it was quite clear his audience loved it too.

Entertainment experts were beginning to cite him as one of the performers who really did have what it takes. "In an industry full of teenage talent show wannabes whisked from obscurity to full-on fame, Bruno stands out as someone who's spent years honing his skills," says Lizzie Catt, diary editor at the *Daily*

Express. "His life has been steeped in music and he started learning the importance of performance at the tender age of three – a tremendous advantage. Those valuable years behind the scenes learning what makes a hit record while writing successful tracks for other artists means he knows what sells – and how far he can go with his own music. His adaptability, unapologetic embrace of many musical genres and ability to surprise his fans hints at a bright future ahead. And while not every critic will applaud him on every twist and turn of the journey, the years since *Doo-Wops & Hooligans* have seen him build up a strong fanbase that will carry him a long way."

Meanwhile, Bruno's personal life looks secure. Although there have been the odd rumours of a break-up with Jessica, at the time of writing the couple seem more settled than ever, with Bruno talking openly about his desire to get married and have children. He had his high living stage when he first moved to Los Angeles and given the closeness he shared with his own parents, he clearly wants to replicate that with children of his own.

And then there's the music. Bruno has got through the tricky second album stage and toured extensively to promote it, adding new dates to his Moonshine Jungle tour as 2013 wore on. After that it would be back to the studios to prove himself once more with a third album. His Hooligans continue to support him, even as people like Philip start to carve out their own solo career, while for Bruno there remains all to play for. In just a few short years, he has emerged as one of the music industry's most dazzling stars.